EDITOR: MARTIN WINDROW

OSPREY MILITARY

MEN-AT-ARMS SERIES 228

AMERICAN WOODLAND INDIANS

Text by
MICHAEL G JOHNSON
Colour plates by
RICHARD HOOK

First published in Great Britain in 1990 by
Osprey, a division of Reed Consumer Books Ltd.
Michelin House, 81 Fulham Road,
London SW3 6RB
and Auckland, Melbourne, Singapore and Toronto

British Library Cataloguing in Publication Data
Johnson, Michael G.
    The American woodland Indians.—Men-at-arms
series, v. 228).
    1. Eskimoes & North American Indians, history
    I. Title   II. Series
    970.00497

ISBN 0 85045 999 0

Filmset in Great Britain
Printed through World Print Ltd, Hong Kong

Author's & artist's note
Michael Johnson wishes to dedicate his work on this
book to the memory of Albert Dennis Burdett and
Dr. James H. Howard.
Richard Hook wishes to dedicate the paintings in this
book to the memory of his good friend, Ronald
Embleton.
Acknowledgements
Grateful thanks to René Chartrand, Gerry Embleton
Robin Golden-Hann, Badger and Dawn Kirby,
William A. Merklein and Ian M. West.

American Woodland Indians

Introduction

In 1492 Columbus discovered the Americas for Europeans, although contacts had probably occurred before this time. He was searching for a western route to the Indies, and hence the term 'Indian' was adopted mistakenly to designate the indigenous American race. However, their origins were in Asia, having crossed into North America, perhaps beginning 30,000 years ago, via the Bering Straits. Ethnologists have divided North America into recognisable culture areas in which the various tribes developed generally similar skills and lifestyles derived from a common environment. These 'cultural areas' are quite arbitrary, and on close examination tribal differences become so apparent that this tool for classification breaks down except in its very widest sense.

The so-called 'Woodland' cultural area has at various times been assigned to all the tribes living east of the Mississippi River between the Gulf of Mexico and James Bay. These can be sub-divided into the south-eastern cultural area; a north-eastern Woodland area encompassing the region between latitudes paralleling the Cumberland and Ottawa rivers; and the eastern sub-Arctic between the Ottawa and James Bay. Our study approximates the middle area and the adjacent parts of the other areas where they are similar or significant.

Historically the area is the most important in the development of the early United States, and the tribes in this region played the most important rôle of all the native Americans in shaping the New World's history. Some historians have suggested that French, not English, would have been the language of the United States had not the Iroquois hatred of the French been greater than their distrust of the English at crucial periods of history. Others have claimed that the American Consti-

tution was influenced by Iroquois political skills. In at least three major battles between Indian and Euro-American military forces more soldiers were killed than at that famed battle in the West when Custer lost his command.

A semi-mythological story from the English colony in Virginia tells of the saving of a leading settler, John Smith, captured in 1607 by the

Algonkin man and woman, mid-18th century, from an anonymous watercolour predating 1776. This tribal group, from the Ottawa and Gatineau River valley regions of Quebec, were wearing trade cloth clothing by this date, retaining native moccasins. This and the associated paintings of Abenakis and Hurons show colours as solid reds and blues. The name of this tribe, of Malecite origin, has been extended to the largest group of linguistically related tribes in North America, the Algonkians. (City of Montreal Archives)

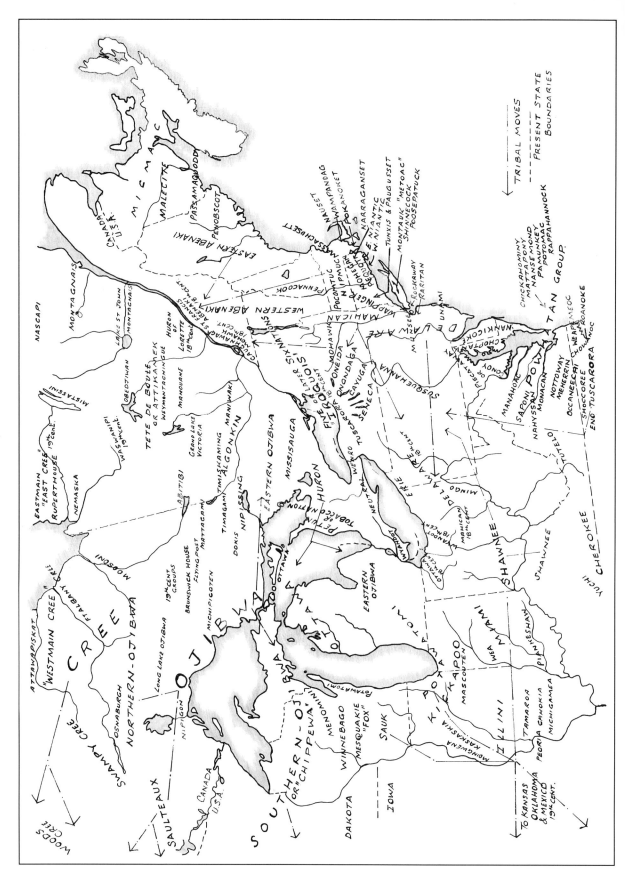

Chieftain Powhatan, by the chief's daughter Pocahontas. It continues with her marriage to John Rolfe, her conversion to Christianity, and her death in England in 1617. She thus seems to legitimise the Anglo-American presence in the New World, and the way to oblivion for her race. That did not happen, although the Atlantic coastal tribes who suffered the first European invasion lost the greater part of their population from diseases and war resulting from contact with whites.

The Iroquois league, on the other hand, living some hundreds of miles inland, were able to successfully come to terms with the white man, given a few generations more to work out political and military adjustment to the new arrivals. The traditional founders of the league were Deganawidah and Hiawatha, the latter subsequently transformed by the poet Longfellow. The legendary purpose behind the confederacy is phrased as a desire to unite warring brother nations. The story tells that five tribes conferred under the 'Tree of the Great Peace', a conference declined by their neighbours, who consequently became potential enemies. The formation of the league is thought to have occurred just prior to the arrival of the white man in the New World. The Iroquois confederacy destroyed and controlled many tribes, establishing itself as the most important native confederacy on the continent, and the nucleus of Woodland culture.

The Woodland Tribes

The popular concept of a tribe as a unified people with common ancestors and political integration does not fit all American tribes. A common language appears the principal criterion to determine a tribe, with sometimes a common origin myth. There are over 50 language families, including a dozen major ones. The major ones represented in the Eastern Woodlands were the Algonkian, Iroquoian, Siouan and Muskogian, the latter in the south-east. (The extinct Beothuk of Newfoundland were an independent language family.)

Location of Indian Tribes in the North-East, 1610–1810. (Author's map)

The Algonkians

Micmac The Algonkian people of Nova Scotia, Cape Breton Island, Prince Edward Island and New Brunswick. Amongst the first people encountered by Europeans in the late 15th century, constantly visited by explorers and fishing vessels, they became firm allies of the French, with whom they greatly mixed. Hostile to English settlers until 1779. Never deported, they have continued to occupy fragments of the ancient homeland until today. Original population 5,000, and now exceed this figure.

Malecite (Maliseet) and Passamaquoddy Two tribes split after the colonial wars, one in New Brunswick, Canada (Malecite), the other in Maine, USA, but basically the same people. Friends of the French; combined population of 2,000; have maintained their numbers, mixed with French ancestry.

Abenaki An important body of Algonkians of Maine in the valleys of the Penobscot, Kennebec, Androscoggin and Saco rivers, including the Penobscot tribe. Close allies of the French and hostile to the English, most of the western Abenakis withdrew to French Canada in the 17th and 18th centuries, except the Penobscot who remained in Maine. They at times formed a confederacy with the Malecite called Wabanaki. The Canadian branch are sometimes called St. Francis Indians.

Pennacook A group of Algonkians on the Merrimac River, New Hampshire. Suffered at the hands of encroaching English colonists, and were involved in the so-called King Philip War, 1675–76. Remnants withdrew to Canada, where they merged with the St. Francis Abenaki.

Massachusett A convenient name to cover a group of Algonkians of present Massachusetts, who came quickly under the influence of the Puritan settlers, who gathered them into villages of 'Praying Indians'. Suffered from smallpox and other diseases. Have disappeared as a people.

Nipmuc A group of Indians of central Massachusetts. Took part in the King Philip War, 1675–76; few survived.

Pocomtuc A small confederacy of western Massachusetts and adjacent Connecticut and Vermont. They joined the hostilities in the King Philip War and at the close fled to Canada or joined other remnant New England groups and disappeared.

Wampanoag, Nauset, Sakonnet A group of tribes

occupying Rhode Island and the south-eastern portion of Massachusetts and adjacent islands. Massasoit, their chief, allowed the settlement of English colonists. His son, Metacomet, or King Philip, led a general revolt of New England tribes, 1675–76. A few survive today in a mixed condition at their settlements at Mashpee and Gay Head.

Narraganset Occupied the greater part of Rhode Island. They helped Roger Williams lay the foundations of that state, and remained on friendly terms with the whites until the King Philip War, when they joined the hostiles and lost over 1,000 killed at the Great Swamp Fight near Kingston. A few mixed with the Eastern Niantic and remain today in their old domain mixed with other races.

Niantic A group usually divided into an eastern branch of Rhode Island closely associated with the Narraganset, and a western branch of Connecticut who were allies of the Pequot.

Hurons-of-Lorette, Quebec, c.1750–80. Some Hurons settled near Quebec in 1697 under Jesuit influence. The couple wear cloth robes, silver ornaments, moccasins, and the woman appears to be holding a wampum belt. (City of Montreal Archives)

Mohegan-Pequot Originally one people, the most important of eastern Connecticut; split into two factions in the early 17th century, one pro- and one anti-English. In 1635 were at war with the Narraganset; in 1637 the Mohegans destroyed the Pequot village near Mystic. Both groups diminished in number under white pressure; several joined other groups and moved to New York state under the name Brotherton. The Mohegans retained a reserve near Norwich until 1861 and have 200 descendants. The Pequots still have two small reserves and number 100 or so of mixed race. Originally they numbered perhaps 3,000.

Montauk or Metoac Names to cover the various small tribes of eastern Long Island; famous for production of shell wampum beads much sought by the mainland tribes. They retained their numbers until 1759, but, ravaged by plagues and crowded out, most moved west in the multi-tribal Brotherton and Stockbridge groups. A few remained on Long Island under names of Shinnecock and Poosepatuck and still number a few hundred.

Wappinger or Mattabesec A name for a number of minor tribes of the western area of Connecticut and the Hudson River valley, New York. Henry Hudson contacted them in 1609. Subsequently crowded out by whites, joined the mixed Brotherton or other tribes and moved west, except for two small groups, the Schaghticoke and Paugusett, who have lingered on in their old haunts until the present time.

Mahican Not to be confused with the Mohegan, these people occupied the Hudson valley north of the Wappinger to Albany. In 1736 their remnants gathered at Stockbridge, Massachusetts, and henceforth were known as 'Stockbridge'. Later they moved to a reservation near the Menomini of Wisconsin; 600 descendants remain.

Delaware or Leni-Lenapi The most important Atlantic coastal tribe occupied the basin of the Delaware River in Pennsylvania, New York, New Jersey and Delaware. There were several sub-tribes, but the important ones were the Munsee and Unami. At first they lived comfortably with the Penn colonists. However, by 1742 they began to move west to the Susquehanna, Allegheny and ultimately the Ohio country, actively engaging in frontier warfare until the Treaty of Greenville, 1795. The

Delaware eventually reached Oklahoma in two groups, one group with the Stockbridge in Wisconsin and three groups in Ontario, Canada. A few mixed-descent people also survive in their homeland. They perhaps numbered 8,000 in the 17th century, and were called 'Grandfathers' by subordinate Algonkian tribes. About 6,000 descendants are still counted.

Shawnee Perhaps historically the most important tribe of the old north-west Ohio country, but their old territory was the Cumberland River in Tennessee. They were a particularly warlike and anti-white frontier tribe. After the Treaty of Greenville they moved to Indiana, where they were involved with the multi-tribal village at the mouth of the Tippecanoe River destroyed by Governor Harrison in 1811. Part of the Shawnee removed to Texas, known as the Absentee-Shawnee during the early 19th century. The Shawnee finally moved to Oklahoma, where three groups still survive. The aboriginal population of the Shawnee was perhaps 6,000; now half that number, and of mixed white ancestry.

Nanticoke The name given to a group of Indian tribes of Maryland and the southern part of Delaware closely related to the Leni-Lenapi. From 1642 to 1678 they were engaged in a dispute with the Maryland colonists. In 1698 reservations were established, but poor conditions forced many to leave for the north, where they merged with the Iroquois. A few remained in their old country.

Conoy or Piscataway An Algonkian people related to the Nanticoke and Delaware (Leni-Lenapi) living in the vicinity of Baltimore, Maryland. Most moved north and merged with the Nanticoke and Iroquois. There are some people in their old country who claim descent.

Powhatan A large Algonkian confederacy located in the Tidewater portion of Virginia from the Potomac River to the James River. There seem to have been 30 major villages and sub-tribes. From

Eastern Great Lakes Iroquois moccasins, 18th century, of single-piece sinew-sewn deerskin construction. There is appliqué and woven porcupine quill-work decoration over the front seam and on the cuffs, which are fringed with tin cones and deer hair. (Capt. Arent Schuyler de Peyster Colln., National Museums & Galleries on Merseyside, Liverpool)

1607 they were in contact with the Jamestown colonists, at which time they numbered 10,000. The term Powhatan refers to the chieftain of the confederacy at the time of the early settlers, who was the father of Pocahontas, who saved the life of a white captive. Two bitter wars with white settlers finally broke them, restricting them to English land grants. Today perhaps 3,000 claim their ancestry under several local names—Pamunky, Chickahommy, Mattaponi and Nansemond—and two old land grants from colonial days survive.

Weapemeoc A tribe of northern North Carolina near the Pasquotank River who maintained themselves until the Tuscarora Wars of the early 18th century.

Chowanoc The large Algonkian tribe of northern North Carolina and the most important south of the Powhatan. At war with English colonists in 1663 and 1675; confined to a reservation in 1707;

Wampum belt, c.1770—tribe unknown. This was collected by Sir John Caldwell when an ensign at Fort Niagara or adjutant at Fort Detroit between 1774 and 1776. (Canadian Museum of Civilization, Ottawa)

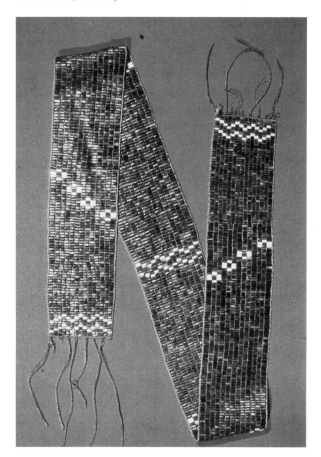

seem to have ultimately joined the Tuscarora.

Moratok, Pamlico, Hatteras, Bear River and Secotan Algonkian tribes in contact with the Raleigh colonists of Roanoke Island, North Carolina, 1585–86. During the 17th century these tribes seem to have re-formed under the name Machapunga near Mattamuskeet Lake, where a reservation existed until the Tuscarora wars. Some mixed descent people have been reported in the area from 1761 until the 20th century. However, there has always been the rumour that these Indians moved inland and are the ancestors of the larger mixed communities of Haliwa and Lumbee and are the fabled Croatan Indians, who are supposed to have adopted the last white people from the Raleigh colony, which ultimately vanished.

Algonkin Group of bands on the upper tributaries of the Ottawa and Gatineau rivers in Quebec, Canada; their name has been adopted to cover the whole language family as Algonkian or Algonquian. Their closest relatives were the Ojibwa. Their history was one of firm friendship with the French from the early 17th century on. Modified in culture by their association with Europeans, but never deported, they have been reported to number 3,000 or so from early days.

Montagnais-Nascapi Two names basically for the same people, who occupied (sparsely) much of northern and eastern Quebec; the northern bands are known as Nascapi, the southern bands along the St. Lawrence as Montagnais. First met by Champlain in the early 17th century, the southern bands have been long associated with French traders and missionaries. Their culture has been modified over the years, although they were always skilful hunters. They are closely related to the Cree. They have been reported to number about 5,500 in 1650 and still number the same today.

Tête-du-Boule or Attikamek Group of Algonkian bands of the St. Maurice River in central Quebec. They are sometimes given Cree status and belong to that section of the great family; their culture was similar to the other sub-Arctic Algonkians. They continue to occupy sections of their former territory. Their numbers have always been about 2,000.

Cree One of the great peoples of the Algonkian

stock and one of the most important of the continent. They expanded from their original territory around James Bay to occupy an area greater than any other North American tribe. Cree importance was due mainly to the position they held in the Canadian fur trade and the influence that position gave them with other tribes. From the early days of their association with the British posts on Hudson Bay they scattered through an immense area; some western bands became Plains indians. They numbered over 25,000 in aboriginal times, and today 80,000, with an equal number of Métis (mixed race), who have Cree ancestry. The sub-Arctic Cree are the Barren Ground Cree, Albany Cree and Moosoni of northern Ontario, and the Swampy Cree or Maskegon of central Manitoba. During the 18th century eastern Cree expanded west into the Saskatchewan country, and became known as the Western Woods Cree. They were able to modify their basic hunting traditions to the new conditions brought by the fur trade.

Ojibwa or Chippewa One of the largest tribes, whose range was formerly on the north shore of Lake Huron, but expanded east and west in promotion of the fur trade from the 17th century on. They finally held an immense broken territory from Quebec to British Columbia, although their homeland core is the Great Lakes. They belong to the northern hunting tradition, but harvesting wild rice, some planting, Feast of the Dead ceremonies show southern influences. In eastern Ontario are the Mississaugas and Nipissing, the northern Ojibwas, who occupied the northern shores of the Great Lakes including, with the Ottawas, Manitoulin Island. The southern Ojibwa of Michigan, Wisconsin and Minnesota are usually called Chippewa. The western expansion of the Ojibwa to Lake Winnipeg and Saskatchewan in the 18th and 19th centuries was due to the fur trade. These people are sometimes known as Saulteaux; a few bands became Plains Indians and are called Bungi. They numbered 20,000 in the 17th century today over 100,000 with an equal number of descendants counted amongst the Métis. However, they always mixed with the European traders and their population is largely of mixed descent.

Ottawa The Indians of Manitoulin Island and northern Michigan. They were friendly to the

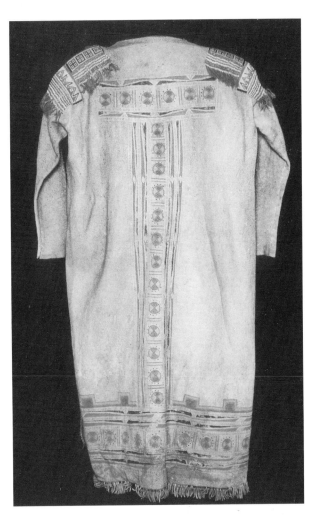

Cree or Northern Ojibwa man's coat, *c.*1770, made from heavy, tanned, unsmoked moosehide. It has epaulettes of woven quill-work, quill-wrapped fringes, and painted designs across the back, round the lower edge, down the front opening and centre back in red, yellow, black and ochre. (Caldwell Colln., Canadian Museum of Civilization, Ottawa)

French and after the destruction of the Huron were often attacked by the Iroquois. They came under French missionary influence and suffered during the colonial conflicts between France and Britain; Pontiac was an Ottawa by birth. A few southern bands moved west and ultimately to Oklahoma; the rest continued in their old territory in Michigan with the main body on Manitoulin Island, where they still remain. Perhaps originally numbering 6,000, today they count in excess of 4,000.

Potawatomi Closely related to the Ojibwa and Ottawa; the ancient home of this tribe was the lower peninsula of Michigan. By 1690 they were at Green Bay, by 1720 in southern Michigan. During the colonial wars in this region they first sided with

Black buckskin pouch decorated with porcupine quill-work, c.1770; the strap is a twined fibre belt ornamented with false embroidery in moosehair. The Thunderbird motifs visible in the lower part of the pouch are among the most popular designs on warrior pouches. (Caldwell Colln., Canadian Museum of Civilization, Ottawa)

the French against the British, then with the British against the Americans. Around 1820 they began to withdraw across the Mississippi and obtained reservations in Kansas and Oklahoma. A few crossed into Ontario, Canada, two bands remaining in Michigan and a few in Wisconsin. They have numbered about 5,000.

Mascouten Group of Algonkians of southern Michigan, later sought protection with the Kickapoo after being almost exterminated by the French. Probably merged with the Kickapoo, Fox and Piankashaws. They are now unknown as a separate people.

Kickapoo Body of Algonkians located during most of the historic period between the Fox and Wisconsin rivers in present Wisconsin or later in the 18th century in Illinois and Indiana. They have always been a conservative and independent nation and, in an attempt to continue so, some moved to Mexico, the rest to Oklahoma and Kansas. They probably numbered 3,000 in early times and, although reduced to 1,000 by 1900, they have since regained their numbers.

Menomini or Menominee This tribe lived during the historic period near Green Bay and the Menominee River, Wisconsin. The main industry of the tribe was the harvest of wild rice, which together with hunting and fishing were the basis of their economy. First known to whites in 1634; quickly under French influence; ceded lands to Americans, and obtained a reservation in 1854 in northern Wisconsin. They have mixed freely with the French and are today mostly of mixed descent, having 4,000 descendants—which was probably their original number.

Sauk (Sac) and Fox (Mesquakie) Two Algonkian tribes whose history and culture have been so close they came to be considered as one. The Fox lived along the river of the same name in Wisconsin and the Sauk originally at Green Bay. They are famous for the stand chief Black Hawk made in 1832 for lands near Rock Island, Illinois. The Sauk finally found a home in Kansas and Oklahoma and the Fox at Tama, Iowa. The latter were, until recently, a stronghold of conservatism.

Illini These Algonkians lived along the Illinois and Mississippi rivers in present Illinois; first contact with French about 1667. Greatly reduced in number by wars with the Iroquois and by smallpox, they reduced from 10,000 to 200 under the name Peoria in Oklahoma. Although the Illini have almost passed from history they have left a strain of their blood amongst many old French families of the Mid-West.

Miami When first known to whites were near Green Bay, Wisconsin, but were on the Kalamazoo River, Michigan, by about 1680, then moved into Indiana along the Wabash and Miami rivers. Prominent in the wars between the British and Americans; their chief, Little Turtle, gained the greatest military victory of a native American leader over American forces in 1791. They suffered as a consequence. They ultimately found homes in Oklahoma under the names Miami, Wea and Piankashaw, formerly sub-tribes; the latter two joined the Peoria. A few continued in Indiana. In 1650 they probably numbered 5,000; today, 500 or so descendants.

The Siouans

Winnebago The only Siouan-speaking enclave within the Algonkian area are the Winnebago of southern Wisconsin. In culture they resembled their neighbours and shared their major religious festivals with the Chippewa and Menomini. They were forced to remove to Nebraska during the 19th century, but many re-established themselves in their old homes in Wisconsin. Both the Nebraska and Wisconsin groups exceed 2,000 people.

Eastern Siouans A number of ancient tribes of northern Virginia, North and South Carolina are for convenience included as the eastern branch of the Siouan language family on largely circum-

stantial evidence—a vocabulary obtained from Tutelo Indian descendants among the Iroquois in Canada in the 19th century, which is thought to be of Siouan extraction. The Tutelo and Saponi with fragmented other groups from Fort Christanna, Virginia, journeyed north to incorporate with the Iroquois in the 18th century. Perhaps the *Monacan, Tutelo, Saponi, Occaneechi, Cheraw* and others can be added to the *Catawba,* of known Siouan extraction, and their possible relatives *Waccamaw,* to complete the eastern branch of the Siouan stock. This formation, however, is by no means without critics.

The Iroquoians

Huron The ancient country of the Hurons was Lake Simcoe, Ontario. The French Jesuits made an enumeration of 32 villages, 700 dwellings, 4,000 families and over 12,000 adult persons. They

Ball-headed clubs from the Eastern Great Lakes region, c.1780. These are of maple wood, with long-tailed animal forms carved on the top of the ball—a feature noted on several ancient clubs, which may perhaps have warrior symbolism. (Museum of Mankind, courtesy the Trustees of the British Museum)

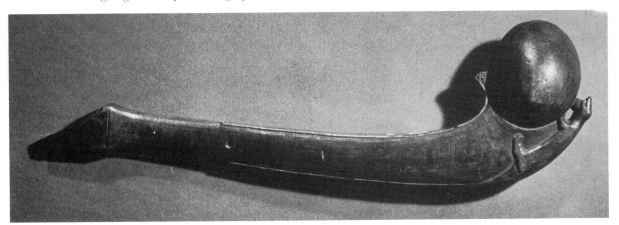

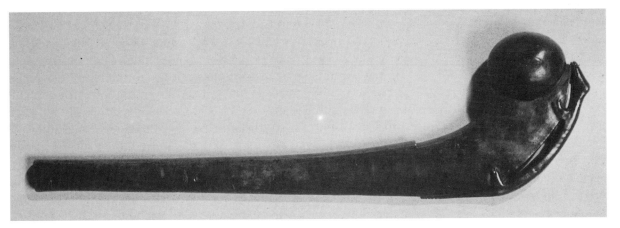

became friends with the French and important in the fur trade. In 1649, to gain control of the fur trade, the Five Nations or Iroquois destroyed their towns and the remnants dispersed westward to the north shore of Lake Huron, even to Green Bay. In the 18th century some returned to French Canada and settled near Quebec city at the village of Lorette. The rest, with remnants of other destroyed Iroquoian groups, lived in the Detroit area under the English name Wyandot. These ultimately then moved to Kansas and Oklahoma. Several hundred mixed-descent people remain from both Lorette and Oklahoma.

Petun, of Nottawasaga Bay, Ontario: *Neutral*, on the north shore of Lake Erie, Ontario: and *Erie*, on the south shore of Lake Erie, in western New York State. Three Iroquoian tribes each in turn destroyed by the Iroquois or Five Nations between 1649 and 1656. Although they disappear from history a few joined the Iroquois by adoption or joined the Huron remnant.

Susquehanna A tribe living along the Susquehanna River in Pennsylvania and New York who were absorbed by the Five Nations during the 17th century.

Five Nations Sometime in the 16th century five Iroquoian tribes of the upper area of present New York State formed a political league. In the early 18th century they were joined by the Tuscarora, a tribe from North Carolina, and henceforth were known as the 'Six Nations'. Today they have 50,000 descendants, twice their former population, but much mixed with Euro-American and other tribal ancestry.

Mohawk The easternmost tribe of the Iroquois league living in the valley of the Mohawk River in east central New York State. Became friends of the Dutch at Albany and later of the British, until more than a third withdrew to French Canada under Jesuit influence and were expelled from the league as a consequence. They fought with the British in the French and Indian Wars and during the American revolution moved over to British Canada. The Mohawk are still the principal people of Six Nations, Ontario; Tyendinaga near the eastern end of Lake Ontario; and the old French contingent at Oka, Caughnawaga and St. Regis, Quebec, now total 10,000, probably twice their old population. The Mohawk chief Joseph

Brant was the leader of the British faction during the late 18th century.

Oneida 'People of the Stone', in allusion to the Oneida Stone, a granite boulder near their former village; a tribe of the Six Nations. They were not loyal to the league's policy of friendliness towards the British, but were inclined to the French. The only tribe to fight with the Americans in the War of Independence. After the war a number migrated to the Thames River, Ontario; the rest later moved to Green Bay, Wisconsin, where a reservation was acquired. They number 5,000 or so, twice their population in olden times.

Onondaga An important tribe of the Iroquois or Five (later Six) Nations, their principal village was also considered the capital of the confederacy. In 1677 it contained 140 cabins and a population of 500 with a total tribal population of 1,700. During the late 17th century the tribe divided; part stayed loyal to the league and the British, others migrated to French Canada under Catholic missionary influence. At the end of the American Revolution some moved to the Six Nations reserve on the Grand River, Ontario, the rest retained a reservation in their old homeland in New York State. Today they number perhaps 4,000, divided between Six Nations, Ontario, the Onondaga reservation, New York, and mixed on several other reservations.

Cayuga Iroquois tribe of Cayuga Lake, New York. In 1660 they were estimated to number 1,500. After the Revolution a large part moved to the Grand River tract in Ontario together with other Iroquois loyal to the British cause. Some also joined the multi-tribal groups in the Ohio country, and joined the Seneca of Sandusky and moved to Oklahoma. Today they have perhaps 2,000 descendants.

Seneca The westernmost tribe of the Iroquois league and the most populous tribe of the confederation, living between the Genessee River and Seneca Lake. Though continually friendly towards the British they remained largely neutral in the American War of Independence—but the Americans still burnt most of their villages. Some moved west into Ohio country, where they mixed with other Iroquois groups under the name Mingo, later Seneca of Sandusky and Seneca–Cayuga of Oklahoma. The majority,

Sir John Caldwell, 5th Baronet, of Castle Caldwell, Co. Fermanagh, Ireland. He served in the 8th (The King's) Regt. of Foot, stationed at Forts Niagara and Detroit, during the early years of the American Revolution. He was elected a chief of the Ojibwa, who gave him the name Apatto or 'Runner'. This painting, by an unknown hand, shows him posing in Indian costume after his return to Ireland. He holds a purple wampum war belt on which an axe motif is woven in white beads. His typical Eastern Ojibwa 18th-century moccasins have tin cone and deer hair fringing. The leggings are of red cloth, the garters woven with interspaced white beads. The black buckskin pouch of Great Lakes types is decorated with quill-work, as is the knife sheath slung across his shoulder. He has several silver gorgets and brooches on his chest and tuban. (National Museums & Galleries on Merseyside, Liverpool)

however, remained in western New York at Cattaragus, Allegheny and Tonawanda, and continue there today. They number probably in excess of 12,000—more than twice their original population.

Tuscarora Iroquoian tribe of North Carolina; a war with the colonists, 1711–13, broke them, and many were subsequently induced north to join the Iroquois league as a sixth nation in 1722. During the revolution part removed to British Canada, where their descendants are amongst the Grand River Iroquois; the rest remained on a reservation near Niagara Falls. However, not all Tuscarora moved north after 1713; some retained a reservation in Bertie County, North Carolina, until 1803 when the last joined the New York Tuscarora. Others are perhaps ancestors of the multiracial groups of North Carolina such as the Lumbee. Today they have perhaps 3,000 descendants in Ontario and New York.

Besides the Iroquoian Cherokee, who are outside the area of the North-East, there were a few other tribes geographically between the northern Iroquoians and the Cherokee. These were the *Meherrin* and *Nottaway* of southern Virginia, *Coree* and *Neusiok* on Pamlico Sound, North Carolina, although it is possible that the latter two were Algonkian.

Burden-strap or 'tumpline', probably Iroquois, 18th century; it is made of twined vegetable fibre ornamented with false embroidery of moosehair in intricate geometrical patterns. (Caldwell Colln., Canadian Museum of Civilization, Ottawa)

Mingo During the 17th century independent Iroquois villages were located in Pennsylvania and Ohio. They were known as Black Minqua or Mingo, and were no doubt a mixture of several tribes. Their place in history is due to a famous chief, John Logan, of supposed French origin but a thoroughly conditioned Indian. After the killing of his family by a mob of white men he carried on a continual war with slender resources against all settlers. About 1800, with reinforcements from the Seneca and Cayuga, they became known as Seneca of Sandusky and in time moved finally to Oklahoma, where a number of descendants remain.

Wars of the Eastern Tribes

Colonial Wars

The first major conflict between the eastern Indians and the white settlers was in present Virginia in 1622–34, and again in 1644. The Powhatan Algonkian groups, under their chieftain Opechancanough, waged war on the Jamestown colonists as the settlement expanded. It is estimated that 650 whites and at least as many Indians were killed.

Further north in southern New England the English colonists, assisted by the Narragansets and Mohegans under the historical Uncas, attacked and destroyed the Pequot fort at West Mystic, Connecticut, in 1637 to crush the influence of their

chief Sassacus, who was resisting English settlement. Over 700 Indians were killed and as many sold into slavery in Bermuda.

Further east, in 1675–78, the power of the New England Algonkian tribes was destroyed during the so-called 'King Philip's War'. For some generations after the settlement of New England the great Sachem (chief) Massasoit had helped maintain an uneasy peace with the Plymouth colonists. However, his two sons, Alexander (Wamsutta) and Philip (Metacomet), were less friendly with the colonists as the seaboard settlements crept inland; the pious pilgrims were gaining converts in many Indian villages and organising so-called 'praying' villages on the perimeter of white domain. Alexander, complaining to the white authorities, was imprisoned and died on his release. As a consequence his brother Philip led the revolt of his own Wampanoag tribes and later of the Narragansets, which resulted in 12 English towns being destroyed, mostly in present Massachusetts. Betrayed by members of his own race Philip lost a major part of his Narraganset warriors at the Great Swamp Fight in Rhode Island, and later, in August 1676, he was killed at Mount Hope. On both occasions his location was given away to the whites by disaffected tribesmen.

The Iroquois confederacy, that unique organisation of central north New York of five separate but related tribes in a league, engaged in a series of wars against neighbouring tribes in the late 1640s and early 1650s. They dispersed or absorbed in turn the Erie, Neutral and Huron to secure the lucrative beaver fur trade with the whites. The so-called 'Beaver Wars' established Iroquois supremacy for the next 130 years of tribal and frontier politics. The Iroquois Mohawks were partly won over to French interest in the late 17th century and moved to Canada, although on the whole the league favoured the British. However, they occasionally attacked English settlements and New England Algonkian villages via the Mohawk Trail over the Berkshire Hills. The remains of northern New England tribes, the Pennacooks and Abenakis, moved to French Canada and joined the Canadian Mohawks in the four major conflicts between France and Great Britain:

(1) King William War 1688–97
The French with their Canadian Indian allies attacked English settlements in New York and New England such as Schenectady, Haverhill and Dover. English counter-attacked.

(2) Queen Anne War 1702–13 ('War of the Spanish Succession' in Europe)
The French again raided English settlements. Famous attack on Deerfield, Massachusetts, 1704, when 48 people were killed and 112 taken captive.

(3) King George War 1744–48 ('War of the Austrian Succession' in Europe)
Continued frontier Indian raids. With Iroquois help the English kept the frontier intact.

Canoe profiles: top to bottom, Micmac, Malecite, Nascapi, Eastern Cree, Algonkin, Ojibwa, Hudson's Bay Company Cree.

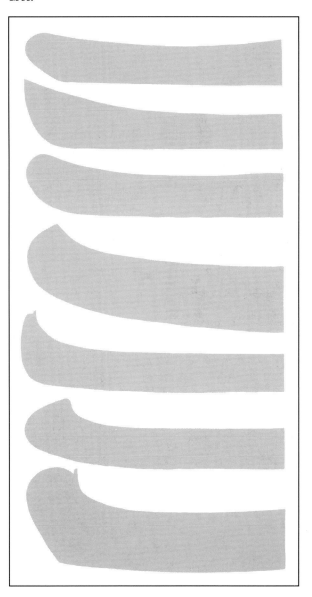

This and the following photographs show reconstructed buildings at St. Marie-Among-the-Hurons, Midland, Ontario, which are based on 17th-century descriptions and archaeological finds. This detail of the doorway of a large elm bark longhouse shows the construction—criss-crossed withies over elm bark sheets. (Robin Golden-Hann)

(4) French and Indian War 1754–63 ('Seven Years War' in Europe)

The English attempted to break French control of the vast area beyond the Allegheny Mountains. Gen. Edward Braddock's ill-fated attempt to capture the French Fort Duquesne (later Fort Pitt) in 1755 ended with an Indian ambush which totally defeated his command; the British lost 900 men and large amounts of provisions and horses. The French captured Forts Oswego and William Henry in 1756; but the British finally captured Fort Duquesne in 1758, followed by Forts Niagara, Ticonderoga, Crown Point, and ultimately Quebec, 1759, and Amherst took Montreal in 1760.

For the most part in these wars the Algonkian refugees from New England, with Catholic mis-sionized Mohawks, were firm French allies. Most of the western woodland tribes—Ottawa, Ojibwa, Potawatomi and Shawnee—were also allies of the French. However, the Iroquois for the most part fought on the side of the English, in part due to the influence the British Superintendent of Indian Affairs, Sir William Johnson, enjoyed among the Mohawk who had remained in their old homes in the Mohawk Valley; the alliance was sealed by his marriage to the sister of Joseph Brant, the Anglicanised Mohawk chief. The Irish trader George Croghan, in the British service of Sir William Johnson, won over the friendship of the western Indians at a great council at Pittsburgh in 1758. In 1761 the British finally took control of the French forts and the Great Lakes area, following the French surrender at Montreal in 1760.

The American Revolution 1775–83

The Iroquois who had been allies of the British were divided by the Revolution. Brant's Mohawks fought for the British and withdrew to Canada at the close of the war. The Tory American John Butler used Indian auxiliaries in the battles of Wyoming and Cherry Valleys. Iroquois who had remained neutral, mostly Senecas, had their villages and crops burned by American Gen. John Sullivan in western New York State. Although a few Iroquois aided the crown during the War of 1812, the power of the Iroquois collapsed at the outcome of the American Revolution and they went into decline. However, such was the unique organisation of the league that they politically revitalised on the Grand River reserve, Canada, where all six tribes were represented; and a renewed religious movement inspired by Handsome Lake, a Seneca divine, allowed the Iroquois to adapt to new conditions despite their loss of lands.

Frontier Wars

The Conspiracy of Pontiac

In 1762 a prophet appeared amongst the Delaware who preached a political union of all Indian tribes and a return to the old Indian life. In a form to be repeated several times in successive years by various divines, this unknown prophet claimed instructions from the Master of Life, which were written down on a series of wooden sticks or symbolic parchments. (Seventy years later a Kick-

General view of the Huron longhouse. (Robin Golden-Hann)

apoo prophet, Kenakuk, inspired another nativistic movement showing strikingly similar use of prayer sticks and heavenly maps indicating the continuity of aboriginal ideas.) Although the prophet is unknown, the Ottawa chief Pontiac took advantage of the movement's pro-French and anti-British feelings and intertribal links to weld a confederacy against the British newcomers into the old North-West. It is estimated that Pontiac's army consisted of 870 warriors—Potawatomi, Huron (called Wyandot by the British), Ottawa, Ojibwa and Mississauga. Pontiac's uprising should be considered a war for Indian independence rather than a conspiracy.

The British military occupied abandoned French posts and their traders replaced French traders who had integrated into Indian society. The British refused to continue the French custom of giving presents to the Indians each year, and this seems to have sparked the frontier war of 1763, the so-called 'Conspiracy of Pontiac', in which every British post between Michilimackinac and Western New York (except Detroit) was seized by Pontiac. A tragic massacre occurred at the Michilimackinac post following a game of lacrosse between native teams watched by the fort's occupants, who foolishly opened the gates, giving Pontiac's warriors access. However, the rebellion collapsed in the fall of 1763, and the tribes dispersed. Acts of torture and cannibalism during drunken celebrations after victories drew criticism from some Indian leaders and from the religious leaders who had argued for a war against the British newcomers. In 1764 Col. Bouquet led a British expedition to the Ohio country and returned to Fort Pitt with 200 released white prisoners. Finally Croghan persuaded Pontiac to Oswego, New York, for a formal peace council with Sir William Johnson in 1766, and hostilities ended. Pontiac was murdered in 1769 by an Illinois Indian. The treaty of Fort Stanwix, 1768, established the Ohio as the boundary between the Indians and the British. The Indians of the Great Lakes still numbered 80,000 at that time, but the following 50 years saw their destruction except for the people in the more northerly remote regions.

Lord Dunmore's War 1774

Shawnee, Delaware, Wyandot and Mingo (Western Iroquois) raided settlers in the southern Ohio River valley and into Kentucky. The Indian country was violated in turn by a series of incursions from the south and east by Virginians in 1774

(Lord Dunmore's war) and American strikes during the Revolution against Delaware, Shawnee, Seneca, Sauk and Fox.

The Old North-West Wars 1790–94

With the French and now the British gone from the old North-West the Indians were faced with American expansion following the Revolution, in which the tribes generally ranged themselves on the British side. The Indians claimed the Ohio country by virtue of solemn treaties, but settlers had already occupied western Pennsylvania, western Virginia and Kentucky. The Americans refused to be bound by treaties of a government against which they had recently successfully rebelled.

With British help from Canada, Little Turtle of the Miami twice defeated American armies, under Harmar in 1790 and St. Clair in 1791. However, the loose confederacy of chiefly Miami, Ottawa, Chippewa and Potawatomi was crushed by the forces of Gen. Anthony Wayne at Fallen Timbers near Toledo, Ohio, in 1794. During the concluding peace treaty at Greenville in 1795 a large portion of the Ohio valley, including hunting grounds of Kentucky, were signed away.

Later and smaller longhouse type. (Robin Golden-Hann)

Tecumseh and the Prophet 1811–13

About 1805 another Indian revivalistic movement was begun by a Shawnee Indian in Ohio. He became known as The Prophet, or by his new name Tenskwatawa, 'The Open Door'. In common with earlier movements he claimed to be the bearer of a new revelation from the Master of Life. Besides preaching against white influences he also exhorted against Indian practices he claimed to be disruptive to tribal life, such as witchcraft and the magic arts. He managed to learn an eclipse of the sun was to take place in the summer of 1806, and his fame and followers spread as his proclamation of this event was confirmed. All except some of his own Shawnee people regarded him as the true prophet and messenger of the Master of Life.

As this intertribal religious movement took hold, the prophet's brother Tecumseh ('Celestial Panther Crouching') formed the movement's political and military confederacy. At a conference with the governor of Ohio in 1807 he fearlessly denied the validity of the Treaty of Greenville of 1795 and declared his intention to resist further white expansion on to Indian lands. His followers were largely Kickapoo and Potawatomi, with varying numbers of other tribes. He later met Governor Harrison of Indiana in August 1810 and

July 1811, and repeated his former claims—to which Harrison replied that the United States would never give up the lands they had bought from their rightful Indian owners by treaty. Tecumseh travelled south to meet the Creek and Choctaw to extend his confederacy, but in his absence and at Harrison's suggestion the American military took the opportunity to break up the prophet's town at Tippecanoe, Indiana, where the new religion had long been centred. The Americans camped provocatively close to the village and subsequently, on 7 November 1811, the Indians attacked by night and were repulsed and dispersed. The Prophet quickly lost the support of his followers, as he had assured them that victory was certain.

When Tecumseh returned from the south his confederacy was in ruins, the remains of the warriors having scattered. As a consequence he joined the British standard on the formal declaration of war in June 1812, and subsequently was killed at the battle at Moraviantown on the Thames River, Ontario, in 1813. The Indian confederacy fought in over 50 military engagements of that war, although pro-British Indians continued to raid American settlements until 1816, when the final dispersal of the last contingent of Indians receiving British military support was achieved, (although annual presents were received by chiefs at Fort Malden, Ontario, until 1842 in recognition of their wartime service). Tecumseh's influence on the southern tribes had been a factor in the Creek war against the Americans, the attack

Wigwams of 'classic' shape, constructed of elm bark and poles; and of a squatter conical outline, made of birch bark. (Robin Golden-Hann)

on Fort Mims in Alabama in 1813 and their defeat at Horseshoe Bend in 1814 by Andrew Jackson. Most of the southern tribes such as the Cherokee had sided with first the French against the British, and then with the British against the Americans during the Revolution. With the defeat of the more northerly conservative Creeks by Jackson some fled to Florida to reinforce the Seminoles in three wars against encroaching Americans in 1816–18; 1835–42; and 1855. The second Seminole war saw the capture of their leader Osceola and his death in captivity, and the forced removal of his people to Oklahoma.

The Black Hawk War 1832

This was an unsuccessful attempt by a portion of the Sauk and Fox tribes known as 'the British band', because of the association with the British since the War of 1812, to keep one of their villages near Rock Island, Illinois. The leader, Black Hawk, was under the influence of a Winnebago visionary and may have been following the earlier example of Tecumseh. On 20/21 July 1832 American soldiers inflicted heavy casualties on the Indians as they attempted to cross the Mississippi. The return of Black Hawk's band to their old village site in Illinois, which had been ceded by a portion of the tribes friendly to the Americans, was considered an 'invasion' by the military. With the exception of the war in Minnesota in the 1860s which involved the eastern branches of the Sioux (who were really only marginally and ancestrally a Woodland people) the Black Hawk War was the last major conflict between strictly Woodland people and the white man.

Warriors and Warfare

Woodland Indian men seem to have revered war above all else and, despite the great message of peace enshrined in the Iroquois league's consti-tution, a conflict between the old men and the young over war policy was endemic. The councils could only adopt a policy of peace or neutrality; they could not force young men to observe it. War had been a major cause of the decline of native population during the 17th century for which the Iroquois compensated by the adoption of captives;

in fact, war parties were often organised for this purpose. So despite the ideal that men were brothers and that killing should stop, the Iroquois were the major native disruptive military force in the North-East.

A warrior who wished to lead a war party would send a messenger with tobacco to ask others to join his expedition. The messenger would explain the purpose of the expedition followed by a ceremonial smoking of the pipe with those who enlisted. Later the warriors arrived near the camp of the leaders, who prepared a feast asking for a final pledge of support. The leader usually appointed lieutenants to act as his aides during the proposed raids. War dances and striking-the-warpost ceremonies were held before the war party left the camp together with a generous supply of 'medicine', and materials for making and repairing moccasins. Amongst many of the eastern tribes parched corn was the standard provision of the warrior on the trail; when mixed with maple-sugar it provided quick sustenance. The final event before the departure of the war party was often the dog feast, which was considered as a final pledge to meet the full fortunes of war.

Dog war feasts were not acts of piety. They were organised by warrior or clan societies in order to receive blessings from spirits. The dogs would be killed, singed, then boiled and prepared in the same way as deer. The meat symbolised the flesh of captives that they might later eat, these enemies being compared to dogs. The attendant cere-monies involving the ritual use of tobacco evoked help from the night spirits and also the bear and buffalo spirits.

On the warriors' journey to the enemy village many songs and dances were held at the nightly camps, the warriors frequently singing of their former victories. The pipe bearer, a noted warrior, often led the war party with the leader walking last. A Chippewa war party would travel 25 miles a day. As the warriors neared the enemy they began preparations for actual warfare: singing medicine songs, making litters for the wounded, and designating individuals to carry extra supplies of medicine, corn and water. An eagle feather banner was often carried by one of the bravest warriors during the fight; another beat a drum to inspire his comrades.

The warriors would array themselves in the most colourful body-painting, trappings, feathers and charms for the attack, which was often made at daybreak after taking ambush positions near the enemy village. The attackers usually rushed the enemy whilst they were sleeping. Occasionally one warrior might inspire the others by making himself a target, throwing away his weapons and clothing as he charged the enemy. Personalised facial and body painting, together with the finest costume and elaborate decoration, were often worn in battle.

Returning victorious war parties sent runners in advance to carry the news of the warriors' approach to their home village. The women would meet the warriors and carry the scalps, painted red, fastened inside hoops on the ends of poles; frequently scalps were given to the women. The women led the procession, waving the scalps and singing, into the village. After the return preparations were made to hold a victory dance, and a feast of dried meat, wild rice and maple sugar followed. The victory or scalp dance seems to have been common to almost every tribe in eastern North America. Wives and sweethearts of warriors usually carried the poles with the attached scalps at celebrations in neighbouring villages. (Unsuccessful war parties were ignored by villagers.)

Amongst the Iroquoian tribes the taking of prisoners was an important part of warfare. They were often adopted into families who had lost warriors in battle, thus helping to maintain population strength. Ceremonial torture of prisoners and the eating of vital organs were also reported by early observers of the Iroquois.

The war dance was usually performed on special occasions such as council meetings to recall past deeds. In the dance itself attitudes of battle, watching, listening, acts of striking the foe and throwing the tomahawk added to the war songs, rapid drumming, recitals and speeches, giving the effect of passion, excitement and violence. Most deeds of valour were recorded by insignia worn in public, usually eagle feathers worn upright, crosswise, hanging down or coloured red. Other warrior insignia were armbands, ankle and knee bands of skunk or otter skin, painted legs, painted hand designs on body or face, and raven's skin around the neck. Sometimes the skulls of slain enemies

Waterway with locks, leading to the river outside the palisade; this gave easy access by canoe to the interior of the town, and was probably used for sanitation purposes as well. (Robin Golden-Hann)

were used as lodge weights, and their flayed skins were used as mats and doorflaps.

The Woodland Indians fought bravely to defend their lands from neighbouring tribes and whites. Their methods of warfare were culturally determined, and any atrocities committed were equally matched by their foes. The torture and burning of captives were often abandoned at the instigation of their own chiefs. Scalping was a New World custom, although it was later much encouraged by the payment of bounties by the English and French. However, killing and scalping were sometimes secondary objectives to prisoner-taking by Iroquois war parties. Scalping for bounty became a feature of white frontier life, as did the severing of heads; King Philip's head was carried to Plymouth at the close of the 1675–76 war, where it was placed on a pole and remained exposed for a generation as a reminder to Indians and whites of the brutality of colonial warfare.

The disruptive use of gifts by both French and British during the 18th century did much to undermine the stability of the frontier and the dependability of Indian auxiliaries. Some of Braddock's Indian scouts reconnoitring Fort Duquesne in 1755 reported few men at the fort. Their leader's son had been killed approaching the British camp despite the fact he had given the proper countersign, and only constant presents had bribed the Indians to continue their duties, with little enthusiasm. The ambush by the French and their Indians of Braddock's army could probably have been avoided by a better understanding and treatment of Indian auxiliaries by the British.

Before the trade tomahawk and gun came into popular use by the Eastern Indians their principal weapons were the bow, the stone tomahawk and the war club. The war club was a heavy weapon, usually made of ironwood or maple, with a large ball or knot at the end. Some antique clubs in museums have a warrior's face carved on the ball, sometimes with inlaid wampum, a long-tailed carved serpent on the top of the ball adjoining the shaft, and a cross motif. The shafts were also sometimes carved with war records and decorated. It appears to have been a devastating weapon at close quarters.

In the Great Lakes region the so-called 'gun stock club' was popular, often having a sharp-pointed horn or steel trade spike at the shoulder. These were largely replaced with the trade tomahawk of English, French or later American manufacture in iron or steel. Originally of a hatchet form, these later incorporated a pipe bowl, thus symbolising a dual rôle in peace and war: to smoke—to parley; to bury it—peace, to raise it—deadly war.

Poisoned blow-gun arrows were used by the Cherokee and Iroquois but not to any extent in the major conflicts, and perhaps for hunting only. Bows were usually of one piece, made from ash, hickory or oak. Arrows had delicately chipped triangular chert heads, and were usually kept in sheaths or quivers of cornhusk or skins. Early reports suggest that a type of wooden slatted

Group of warriors, perhaps Iroquois, c.1815–20: hand-painted lithograph by Dennis Dighton (1792–1827) who was appointed military draughtsman to the Prince of Wales in 1815—the print was published in 1821. The men wear natural-coloured buckskin coats of European cut, braided coloured wool sashes, silver earrings, and feather headdresses, and some hold the long Woodland-style bow, a weapon by now almost obsolete among the Iroquois. (North American Indian Colln., Ulster Museum, Belfast)

English-made pipe-tomahawk, early 19th century. (Ian West Colln.)

armour made of tied rods was used by the Huron and Iroquois.

The gun replaced the bow throughout most of the eastern regions between about 1640 and the late 17th century, and partly rendered obsolete the bow and arrow and rod armour. However, as late as 1842 (due to lack of ammunition) and eyewitness reported that a battle between Chippewa and Sioux was waged with club and scalping knife.

Between the 17th century and early 19th century the practice of warfare changed little. A warrior's equipment in later years included a blanket, extra moccasins, a tumpline used as a prisoner tie, a rifle, powder horn, bullet bag, and his own medicine. Delaware and Shawnee scouts in the US Army in the West are said to have administered warrior medicine to white soldiers. The calumet ceremony was often performed for war and peace. It appears to have been of Mississippian origin and spread east to the Ottawa via most central tribes, together with ritual use of tobacco and steatite and catlinite pipe bowls. Calumets were highly decorated wands of feathers, painted tubes with animal parts, including the heads and necks of birds, with or without the pipe. The use of the calumet and pipe for ritual smoking at treaty councils led to the term 'peace pipe'.

Whilst inter-tribal warfare seems always to have been the norm, the arrival of the Europeans added to inter-tribal rivalry for the fur trade. The Iroquois' conquests seem to have been largely to establish their superiority in the fur trade. About the year 1700 the Iroquois reached the culminat-ing point of their empire. From the start their relationship with the French was difficult, and from 1640 to 1700 a constant warfare was main-tained, broken by periods of negotiated peace, the exchange of prisoners, and periods of missionary influence, which drew a portion of the Mohawks from their homelands to Canada. Their friendship with the English remained largely unbroken dur-ing the 17th century, but during the 18th century frontier politics were such that the league weak-ened and individual tribes no longer acted in one accord with league policy.

The Jesuits had established missions in eastern Canada by 1639, and by 1700 they were as far west as the Mississippi River—thus the French domin-ance of the Great Lakes fur trade until 1761. They forged a link with their southern colony and encircled the English Atlantic seaboard colonies through the western wilderness. However, it was not always a friendly relationship between the French and the various Indian tribes, and several wars involved them with the Mesquakie (Fox), Sauk, Dakota (Sioux), Huron and Chickasaw. At times Indians took their furs to the British posts of the Hudson's Bay Company in the far north, or even to Albany. By the 1730s the focal point of Indian and frontier colonial warfare was the Ohio River country, now populated along its tributaries by tribes forced across the Appalachian mountains by white population pressure. These were princi-pally the Delaware and Shawnee, with portions of

23

many tribes forming a multi-tribal population, including fragments of all six Iroquois tribes now called Mingo; Mahican, New England groups, Abenaki and Chippewa (Mississauga). Tribal alliances usually depended upon the more adequate supplies of trade goods; but the French gradually regained the upper hand in the Indian trade, in part by the use of tribute presents handed to chiefs, and they were in control of the Ohio country at the outbreak of the 'French and Indian War'.

The Iroquois had conquered or exterminated all the tribes upon their immediate borders and by 1680 had turned their arms against more distant tribes, the Illinois, Catawba and Cherokee. According to Iroquois tradition the Cherokee were the original aggressors, having attacked and plundered a Seneca Iroquois hunting party, while in another story they are represented as having violated a peace treaty by the murder of Iroquois delegates. The Iroquois war party usually took 20 days at least to reach the edge of Cherokee territory. Such a war party was small in number as the distance was too great for a large expedition. The Cherokee often retaliated by individual exploits, a single warrior often going hundreds of miles to strike a blow which was sure to be promptly answered by a war party from the north. A formal and final peace treaty between the two tribes was arranged through the efforts of the British agent, Sir William Johnson, in 1768. The peace treaty made at Johnson Hall in New York State appears from the records to have been initiated by the Cherokee.

Although the horse was adopted by the eastern tribes as a beast of burden, there seems to be little reference to its use in warfare except in the later 18th and early 19th centuries and particularly by the western tribes Sauk, Fox, Winnebago, etc. However, the Iroquois and Cherokee had large numbers of horses from the mid-18th century on.

Cradleboard, Northern Ojibwa or Cree, c.1830. Wooden board with curved headbow to protect the infant. The laced front and the style of bead-work on the blue woollen bag which holds the infant indicates manufacture no further south than northern Minnesota; some of the attachments suggest that this example was traded west to the Plains area. (Pitt Rivers Museum, Oxford University)

1: Virginia Algonkian Man, c.1620
2: Carolina Algonkian woman, c.1580
3: Niantic-Narraganset warrior, c.1670

4: Huron warrior, c.1625
5: Mohawk warrior, c.1640
6: Algonkian woman, St. Lawrence Valley, c.1630

A

1: Iroquois warrior, c.1759
2: Mohawk warrior, c.1710
3: Mohawk warrior, c.1764

B

1: South-eastern Ojibwa warrior, c.1800
2: Miami warrior, c.1790
3: Wyandot chief, c.1780

C

1: Shawnee warrior, c.1790
2: Northern Ojibwa warrior, c.1780-1800
3: Cree women, c.1780-1800

2a

1

2

3

D

1: Micmac couple, c.1820
2: Salteaux family, c.1810
3: Details

E

Iroquois, 1800-1820
1: Woman
2: Warrior, War of 1812
3: Dancer

F

1: Sac (Sauk) chief, c.1830
2: Sac woman, c.1830
3: Sac chief's son, c.1830

4: Bark houses
5: Ottawa chief, c.1815
6: Winnebago warrior, c.1820

G

1: Menomini woman, c.1850
2: Sac chief, c.1845
3: Huron-of-Lorette man, c.1845
4: Southern Ojibwa (Chippewa) man, c.1865

H

Woodland Indian Life and Culture

The so-called Woodland Indian culture area was an ever-changing blend of ancient cultural traditions developing distinctive processes of skills, art and religions.

In about AD 500 the 'Mississippian' culture developed. This 'temple mound' period, c.AD 700–1700, is characterised by intensive agriculture of a meso-American type, relatively superior pottery, palisaded fortified villages, flat-topped pyramid mounds (cahokia), and villages which traded obsidian from the Rockies, shells from the gulf, and mica from North Carolina. During the 15th century a religious cult—the 'southern cult', with associated ritual objects—was grafted on to the existing temple platform traditions. The explorer De Soto's expedition of 1540 saw the dying remnant of Mississippian culture as it survived amongst the Cherokee, Creek and Natchez.

The northern offshoot of this culture, a provincial Mississippian influence, was the core of eastern Woodland culture. The Feast of the Dead witnessed by French Jesuits amongst the Iroquoian Huron of Ontario relates to Mississippian culture. The Iroquoian-speaking Huron were the northern limit of extensive agriculture, albeit crude.

Iroquois Culture and Religion

The Iroquois or Five Nations were also part of this Woodland tradition, and were a league welded together from the Mohawk, Onondaga, Oneida, Cayuga and Seneca tribes, with the Tuscarora added later. This league appears to have been drawn from warring tribes joined for defence. The Iroquois were always on terms of chronic hostility with several tribes separated by large distances, e.g. the Catawba and Cherokee of the south and Ojibwa and Sioux of the west, apart from their involvement in colonial conflicts and the fur trade.

The Iroquois calendrical agricultural ceremonies that play such an important rôle in the later descriptions of Iroquoian life may post-date the fall of the Huron. Perhaps warfare and human sacrifice customs that we know from Jesuit sources gradually died out as the fur trade replaced warfare as a prime activity. Certainly the ceremonial eating of human vital organs does not seem to have existed in the late 18th century. However, curative medicine societies and festivals from their agricultural yearly cycle predominate later Iroquois religious life.

Their religion was dualistic: the object was to please spirits both friendly and unfriendly. Their creator, Orenda, who embodied the health and creativity of nature, was opposed by the evil and destructive spirits which had to be appeased. The most famous medicine society, but not originally the most important, were the False Faces, whose masks were sometimes carved from a growing basswood tree. They represented disembodied beings, and when they were worn by society members, the sick were healed by blowing on them through the mouths of the masks. Some healing traits are thought to be indirectly the influence of white Christians, who influenced the important Indian ceremonialist named 'Handsome Lake', a Seneca who at the close of the 18th century re-organised Iroquois religious life.

Iroquois preoccupation with the dead (or one aspect of it—the condolence of mourners) was a survival from ancient times. Condolence rituals cleansed those in despair at the loss of a chief or family member. The object was to refocus compassion on survivors to reduce sorrow and, in the case of a chief, to raise up a successor.

The entire process of planting, cultivating, harvesting and preparation of food was in the hands of women; their leaders, called Matrons, held important positions in Iroquoian society, together with the male Faith Keepers. The ceremonial spirits of maize, beans and squash were called 'Our Life' or the 'Three Sisters'. The range of Iroquoian agricultural produce is impressive: hominy, succotash, ten varieties of beans, black-berries, blueberries and cranberries provided popular dishes. The Iroquois raised fields of corn (maize), beans and squash flanking their semi-permanent villages, which assured a supplementary food supply to meat, but these crops were vulnerable to destruction by enemies.

The Iroquois built elm bark longhouses up to 100 feet long, sheltering up to 20 families. Plat-

Major Indian Wars in the North-East

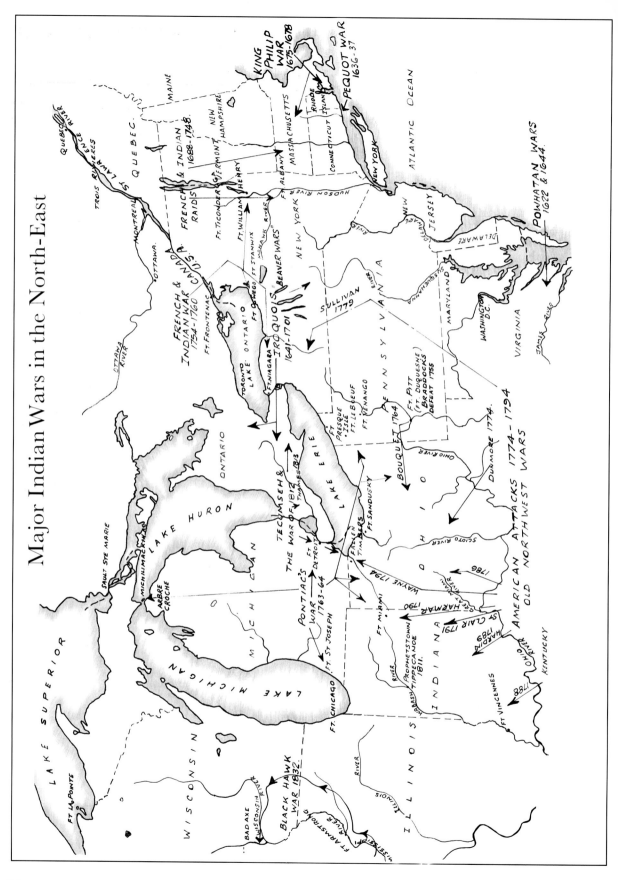

forms along the sides provided sleeping alcoves. Longhouses were usually built by men but owned by women, and were sometimes surrounded and protected by a stockade. During the 18th and early 19th centuries bark dwellings were replaced by log cabins of the Euro-American frontier type, a few of which were still found on Iroquois reservations in the early 20th century. The overcrowding of these longhouses was recalled by the Jesuits who lived among the Huron. In later times the longhouse became a building in which conservative religious practices took place, and hence present-day traditional Iroquois folk are often referred to as 'longhouse members'. (There is still a sizeable membership of the Handsome Lake-inspired Longhouse religion at Oshweken, Ontario, and elsewhere the greencorn, midwinter and harvesting rites continue each year.) Connected with farming were the Corn Husk Faces, another mask-making society whose members served as messengers of the Three Sisters and represented farmers from the other side of the world who visited during the midwinter rites.

Compared with their ceremonial and political life, the Iroquois' arts were less developed. Pottery was crude; but decorative arts, porcupine quill, animal hair and bead embroidery prospered among them in many forms, with designs of celestial, geographical and mystical phenomena. A number of antique pouches, moccasins, tumplines and so-called 'prisoner ties' have survived the ravages of time to bear testimony to their skill and dexterity.

Wampum

Wampum and wampum belts were also strongly associated with the Iroquois and others. Wampum were beads cut from the shell of the clam (purple) or conch (white) of the Atlantic coast or large rivers, cylindrical in shape rather than globular; the two colours were rated at specific values. Wampum was manufactured by the coastal tribes and traded to the interior peoples for use in necklaces, but its most important use was when woven into belts with designs either pictographically or symbolically commemorating public occasions. In ancient times a treaty was not considered binding without the presentation of wampum belts, which were also frequently used as a standard of exchange by Indians and whites. Later the

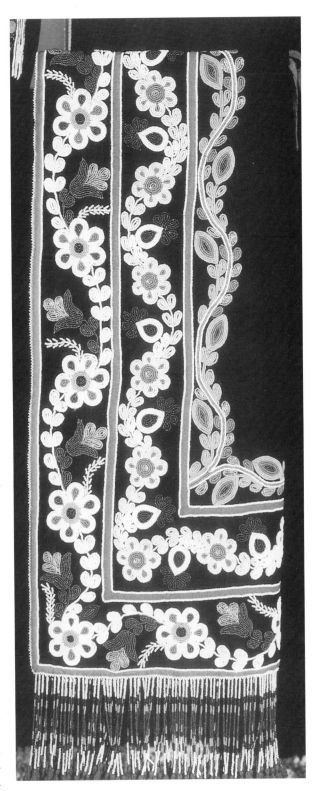

Woman's hood, Cree, *c.*1860. Made from black broadcloth, it is heavily decorated with floral bead-work in a style usually attributed to the Ontario Cree, but was collected from Indians in Saskatchewan, indicating how widely decorated costume items were traded. (Lower Fort Garry Museum, Manitoba)

35

Mittens, Eastern Cree, c.1840s. Of caribou hide, they have silk-embroidered floral designs—silk thread replaced animal hair for embroidery in many regions. (City of Sheffield Museum, MGJ photograph)

Dutch settlers made their own wampum for trade and native-made wampum fell into disuse.

Algonkian Culture and Religion

More widespread in the boreal forest were the many tribes of the Algonkian family, primarily a linguistical family of the north, but which also held most of the coastal plain as far south as North Carolina. Some tribes were probably descendants of people of the northern and eastern perimeters of the old Mississippian culture. The coastal and interior Algonkians, except for those of Canada, were semi-agricultural, and we have a pictorial view of what their homes and villages looked like from the drawings made at Secotan and other villages by the artist John White in 1587. He shows warriors' and women's dress, wigwams, farming, fields, and ritual ceremonials perhaps depicting 'striking the post'. Unfortunately, most of these coastal Algonkian people were either destroyed or drastically changed by the invasion of the Europeans in the 17th century, and almost nothing of their material culture has survived.

However, the core of forest Algonkian life and culture were the Ojibwa or Chippewa, really three tribes very closely related: Potawatomi, Ojibwa and Ottawa. From their relatively narrow location north of Lake Ontario, following the destruction of the Huron, they had by the early 19th century expanded through most of present Michigan, Wisconsin, Minnesota, Ontario, southern Manitoba and the whole of the Great Lakes area in their pursuit of the advantages associated with the fur trade. In many areas around the Great Lakes existence was partially based on collecting wild rice as an annual harvest. The wild rice areas were a constant source of dispute between the Chippewa (Southern Ojibwa) and the Santee or Eastern Sioux, whom they gradually displaced. The western expansion of the Ojibwa and their northern cousins the Cree through their general involvement in the fur trade was of major importance in the rearrangement of many western woodland and plains tribes.

The Ojibwa shared the Feast of the Dead ceremonial complex reported by the Jesuits living with the Huron, a Mississippian-type burial festival; and, in common with the Iroquois, a curative image pervades later Ojibwa ceremonial life as expressed in the Grand Medicine society or Midewiwin. In briefest terms, the Midewiwin was a set of ceremonials usually conducted in a long, open-ended bark lodge, organised by male priesthood and, amongst the Chippewa, by women priests as well. Membership in the 'Mide' society was limited and graded, the various degrees requiring initiation and payment. Its probable geographical centre was La Pointe or Chequamegon. The central feature of the Mide ceremony was the 'shooting' of candidates with a medicine pouch containing the curative and sacred *megis*, a medicine arrow—in reality a shell. The candidate collapses as if dead and is revived by the priests. The 'rebirth' secures health and long life.

The Ojibwa world view was characterised by an overwhelming fear of sorcery and they had a pantheon of destructive spirits (such as the Windigowan, giant forest cannibals formed of Ice), the complete natural world being inhabited by spirit forms. As with the Iroquois, the Ojibwa have a belief in a supreme spirit, Manito or Midemanido, and had a great culture hero, Nana-bush. Some Ojibwa folkloric traditions are recorded in pictographic form on birch bark rolls. The 'Mide' was also important amongst the Menomini, Sac, Fox, Winnebago, some bands of Cree, amongst the Prairie Algonkian, where it is known as the

Medicine Dance, and amongst the Siouan Omaha, the Shell Society. All have the featured 'shooting element' and resurrection, and in all these tribes shamans had a unique and feared position in tribal society.

The deeply religious world of the Woodland peoples was inhabited by supernatural beings, the spirits of the animals, plants, sun, sky and rocks from whom the Indians sought guidance through prayer and fasting. A dream was often interpreted as a message from a spirit to the dreamer, giving him supernatural protection or power. A young man might pass days alone without food or water seeking a vision from some unknown being, which could become his guardian spirit and protector for life. A man who gained several spirit helpers and more supernatural powers became a shaman. Hunters and warriors would consult a shaman before setting out on expeditions.

After a winter of hunting and trapping in small family groups, nomadic central Algonkians gathered in springtime to tap the maples and boil the sap down to hard sugar. The band would then move on to their summer village for a communal summer of fishing and gathering wild crops. Wild rice and corn were North America's only native food grains. Each September the Chippewa Indians of the upper Great Lakes gathered, dried and stored great quantities of wild rice. They paddled canoes through shallow water knocking the grain from the stalks into the canoes. The birch bark canoe was light and well suited for travel by rivers and lakes separated by narrow pieces of land, over which they could be carried on the shoulders of one or two men. Others would carry back packs by tumpline across the forehead. The whole exercise of crossing from one river or lake to another was known as portage.

The Delaware of the Atlantic coastal area shared with the Iroquois the display of their ceremonial life in a special longhouse they called the Big-House. They too had a mask complex, which extended in some form—either post masks or the usual facial type—south to the Cherokee.

The Shawnee shared some of their religious complexes with the South-East; the most important festival which has survived through historical times was the Green Corn celebration or 'Busk' as it is called amongst the Creek. This maize festival was part of a religious complex extending from the Seminole of Florida north to the Iroquois. The celebration was an occasion for amnesty, forgiveness and absolution of crime, lasted four to eight days, and was held in a town square (or now, amongst the conservative Oklahoma Creek, a square dance ground). The ceremonial, which involved the taking of a black drink which resulted in vomiting to ceremonially cleanse the body, revolved around the lighting of the new fire with logs at cardinal points, a world renewal complex of Mississippian origin. The persistent religious colours of red for blood and war and white for peace are evident throughout South-Eastern ceremonialism.

The Shawnee, like many related tribes, believed that their world was an island balanced on the back of a Great Turtle and supported at its corners by four enormous spirit snakes. The island, with all

Cree moccasins of moosehide, probably from one of the western groups; they retain the leg extension typical of the forest and sub-Arctic Cree but examination reveals the side-seam construction found on the north-eastern perimeter of the Plains and 'parklands'. This poor photograph does show the leg extensions, and the bead-work decoration which appears to be the sun motif often repeated throughout the northern forests. (Museum of Mankind, courtesy the Trustees of the British Museum)

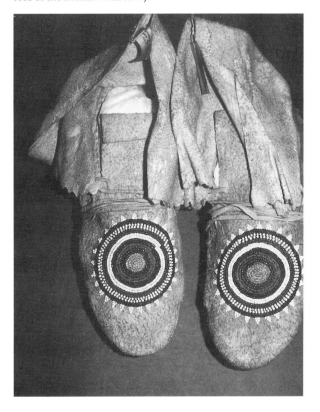

Indian chief of the Six Nations, *c.*1860s; photographer unknown. Note the nose ring and painted moustache; the beaded baldric worn over the buckskin jacket; and the beaded cap decorated with feathers and (?) horsehair—according to the late Dr. James H. Howard this was a type of headdress worn and remembered by the Oklahoma Seneca-Cayuga Iroquois descendants.

its peoples, all things in it, even the heavens above, were believed to be the work of a creator spirit sometimes called the Finisher; the Shawnee were unique amongst Algonkian peoples, however, in believing that their creator was a woman. During the time of Tenskatawa's teachings prior to the War of 1812 one of several reasons why most Shawnee refused to accept and follow his prophecies was perhaps his attempt to remake the creator spirit into a male image. However, by this time the Shawnee were already a fragmented people. Tenskatawa (the Prophet) and his brother Tecumseh, the military and political organiser of the inter-tribal confederacy which opposed American settlement of the Ohio valley and the Great Lakes, although both Shawnee, recruited relatively few of their own tribesmen to the confederacy. As early as the 1670s Shawnees were dispersed from their tribal territory, the watershed of the upper Ohio River and its tributaries, partly by Iroquois expansion. Some moved west, and a large body moved south into the Carolinas and Georgia under Creek protection. In the 1730s they began to move back into parts of their old territory; however, they never again co-operated as a single people.

The Sub-Arctic Algonkians

The northernmost Algonkian who were primarily hunters were the Nascapi, who were dependent on the caribou, and the closely related Montagnais; the Eastern Cree, Tête-du-Boule, the Algonkian proper, and the Micmac of the Maritimes (plus the extinct Beothuk, probably an unrelated people of Newfoundland). The north, as a whole, is characterised by extremes of climate accompanied by seasonal fluctuations in resources. The topography ranges from forest to lake, swamp, prairie, tundra, mountain and sea. The winters are long and freezing; the summers short, hot, humid, and accompanied by a dense insect life which was difficult for man and animal alike.

Northern Canadian Algonkians also hunted deer and elk, constructed fine bark canoes and snow shoes, and were divided into small bands with few community ceremonies. Strong shamanist belief in a world of game spirits prevailed. A culture hero called Glooscap was a joker and trickster who went about as a benefactor of mankind, although there were some monsters he could not conquer, such as the Witigo cannibal ice giants. Amongst the north-eastern Algonkian settled life was possible for only part of each year. In the summers they gathered at fishing grounds

'To Keep the Net Up', a Chippewa (Ojibwa) chief, c.1860s, photographed by Whitney & Zimmerman, St. Paul. He has a braided wool sash across his shoulder, and appears to be holding a knife and warclub with fur decoration denoting warrior status. His coat appears to be made of Hudson's Bay blanket cloth.

and gathered or traded corn in the southern regions during the fall.

The Fur Trade

The fur trade was the basis for a unique interaction between Europeans and the indigenous people of America. Europe's desire for the skins of fur-bearing animals, particularly beaver, led to the establishment of several generalised trading systems: the Iroquoian trade of the 17th century in the eastern Great Lakes and Ohio country; the Ojibwa (Chippewa) domination of the Great Lakes area in the 17th and 18th centuries, with the Hudson Bay area dominated by the Cree and Assiniboine; and the 18th-19th-century trans-Mississippi/Missouri trade of the Plains Indians. Many of these Indian people thrived on the interaction with Europeans through the exchange of technology, communication, material objects and development of political relationships. Their population today, Assiniboine excepted, is far greater than in aboriginal times. The association led to a shift in geographical distribution, as well as social and religious customs. Intermarriage with frontier 'voyagers' of European origin—mainly French or British—led to the emergence of the Métis. The fur trade lasted 300 years from 1600 to 1900 or so in more remote areas, and opened the way for illicit alcohol trade, disease, and the other negative by-products of European contact and influence.

Modern historians, however, do not believe these influences were as significant to the destruction of old Indian life as once thought. Indeed, the remote northern fur trading post was more probably the basis for continuation of independent life, retention of kinship patterns and language; the development of colourful and elaborate stitchery in beads, quills and silk thread for commercial gain; and other conservative traits. The Indian was rarely the conservator of natural resources he is often portrayed by modern popular myth, but rather an adaptor and innovator.

Beaver were prized for their flesh and often caught in winter when their fur was at its best. Beaver were also sought by the earliest white traders, and the Iroquois expansion in the mid-1600s was a direct result of their desire to secure the beaver fur trade with whites and the consequent urgency of obtaining new hunting grounds. The Northern Algonkians wintered in traditional hunting groups of about 20 people. Moose, bear and deer were shot or speared and smaller animals snared. A moose might be trailed until, harassed by dogs, it was driven to collapse. The animal would be skinned and the meat 'cached' for the women to take back to camp on toboggans. Hunting could be continued through the winter with the aid of snowshoes holding the hunter on top of the deep snow, while the larger game animals were often immobilised or found their manoeuvrability greatly diminished.

The commercial trade between the Ohio Indians and French or British agents and traders during the 18th century was of a different nature: it degenerated into competition for Indian alliances by means of gifts. War gifts of cutlasses, scalping knives, hatchets, guns, powder and bullet moulds were added to vermilion paint, flints, cottons, blankets, scissors, needles, thread, cloth, watch-coats and stockings. Once the Indians had become accustomed to the white man's goods they could not live without them. Unscrupulous traders plied Indians with rum, which often resulted in intoxication, brawls and death. Trade goods were also used to purchase Indian lands unless the Indian lived in the Hudson's Bay Territory, where British policy for many years protected him as a hunter. The British spent £90,000 on presents between 1775 and 1779 in the diplomatic competition with the American revolutionaries for Indian alliances.

Technology, Dress and Art

Wood and bark were the most important materials to the forest Indian. Canoes of birch bark were used by the northern Algonkian tribes. The major tribal canoe types had distinctive shapes in the curve of prow and stern or sheer of the gunwales. The Micmac had ocean-going canoes. Quality birch bark was lacking in the Iroquois area, so elm was used. From New England south canoes were of the dug-out type. Bark canoes were used principally for summer travel, being light and transportable from lake to lake by portage. The canoe had a frame of spruce and cedar wood and the stitched bark joints were sealed with spruce gum. Sometimes the Algonkians painted the prow and stern with protective symbols and designs.

Wood was the basic material for snowshoe frames, toboggans, bows, arrows, paddles, clubs, splint baskets, oval and truncated containers, vessels, spoons, bowls, pestles, mortars, cradle-boards, log water drums, lacrosse racquets and ball game sticks. In the north Algonkians transported goods on snow and ice by hand-drawn toboggans. European dog-breeding introduced dog teams, with sleds or raised runners to replace toboggans. Snowshoes, a significant sub-Arctic winter travelling aid, like canoes had various functional and tribal shapes, and sometimes symbolic designs were added to the rawhide 'babiche' webbing construction to enlist the help of game spirits in hunting expeditions.

Domed and conical wigwams were known throughout the northern forests; sheets of bark, usually birch or elm, were sewn to a sapling frame with spruce roots. South of the large birch area woven mats of reeds were used as an alternative to sheets of bark. The Iroquois used longhouses for several families, the Chippewa used small family wigwams. The Iroquois sometimes had wooden fortifications surrounding a group of longhouses. In many of the activities using wood the white man's 'crooked' knife, refined by native use, was an all-purpose tool, so named because of the upturned end of its single-edged blade; it greatly facilitated the refinement of utilitarian objects made of wood. Such objects were taken up by European traders and became indispensable to their adopted northern life, particularly canoes and snowshoes.

The Indians used all manner of animal hides. In the sub-Arctic caribou was used by Nascapi and Montagnais, moose was common in the boreal forest and commonly used by the Crees, and deer hides were popular with all the northeast tribes. Bear and smaller game skins were all used to an extent, such as marten, hare, rabbit, squirrel, mink, fox, beaver, coon, lynx, otter, etc. black-dyed buckskin was used by many eastern tribes, and significantly, black trade broadcloth and velvet were popular in the late 18th century, suggesting a religious association with black. Bison hide was used for robes by some of the more southern tribes such as the Illini and some fibre bags used woven bison hair; however, by the end of the 18th century bison products seem to have virtually disappeared from eastern technology.

European cloth largely replaced hide as the main clothing material for men and women. Black, blue and red cloths were popular, some imported from England being known as 'strouding'. Plants and roots were used to dye hides, animal hair and porcupine quills for decoration of costume and objects. Indians also boiled cloth to extract European pigment dyes; and after 1850 chemical aniline dyes became available from traders.

The Indians of eastern North America had a long period of white contact and a gradual Europeanisation of their art and technology resulted. The adoption of whites and the multi-tribal reorganisations of the 18th century have resulted in the

Chippewa brave, c.1860s—another study from the series taken by J. E. Whitney of St. Paul, Minnesota. He wears a turban with an eagle feather, a treaty medal, a trade blanket, and holds a pipe.

'hybrid' appearance of many objects now in museums. Before the end of the 17th century flax, wool, cloth, beads, silver, axes and metal objects had invaded Indian villages from the Atlantic to the Mississippi.

We have an incomplete picture of the costume of the Atlantic coastal tribes. Early 16th-century descriptions tell of painted deer robes for men and women and the decoration of ears with hanging ornaments. Later Henry Hudson tells of copper objects used as pipes and neck ornaments, suggesting European trade contacts. Early reports and sketches show tattooing, snakeskin or wampum turbans, scarlet deer hair headdresses (roaches), hide tunics and skirts for men and for women. Leg-length caribou and moose hide tunics and coats survive in museum collections from the northern sub-Arctic Nascapi, Cree and Ojibwa, and were probably well known to the Micmac, Iroquois and others. Although many surviving examples have European refinements in cut and shape and display sophisticated painting, they are no doubt

Chippewa chief White Cloud, c.1860s. Eagle and turkey feathers are worn in the hair, and his face is painted, probably indicating warrior status; he wears a Hudson's Bay trade blanket. Whitney & Zimmerman photograph.

native in basic construction; however, early native styles may have been loose and less tailored. The Métis are thought to have developed the tunic into its most baroque and European form in the 19th century. Buckskin shirts have also been collected from the Ojibwa and Winnebago, but again quite tailored, suggesting some European influence. By the 18th century coats and shirts were often constructed of broadcloth and calico. Leggings for men were folded tubes of buckskin (or, by the 18th century, broadcloth or strouding) with ties to a belt at the top. A rectangular buckskin or cloth breechcloth was looped over a belt back and front. We know from material in our museums that men also used pouches, knee garters, sashes, turbans, mittens, and necklaces of wampum and bear claws. Amongst the more western and southern Woodland groups a legging construction was sometimes used where the seam in the tube runs down the front of the leg instead of along the outer edge. Throughout the east there are many references to headdresses, usually bands of cloth or buckskin with upright feathers, so we can speculate

on an ancient origin. Hoods were also used in the north-east and sub-Arctic.

The earliest woman's dress was the slit calf-length wrap-around deerskin skirt, later made of cloth, usually without any upper body cover. In later years calico blouses with ruffled collars became popular, also knee-length cloth or calico dresses. In the more northerly regions a dress with straps over the shoulders and separate sleeves was used, particularly by the Nascapi, Ojibwa and Cree. Amongst the Crees close to the plains the rare hide side-fold dress was used. In recent times the cloth skirt and blouse have been used by Oklahoma descendants of eastern tribes. Southern Ojibwa (Chippewa) women have favoured a cloth dress with hundreds of tin cones attached, known as a jingle dress, for ceremonials and pow-wows.

Moccasins for both men and women were of three main types. In the more southern regions and on the coast the single one-piece hide moccasin with a front seam over the instep to the toe appears to be the ancient form. In the eastern sub-Arctic area a separate 'vamp', a U-shaped piece of hide, is used over the instep and sewn to the body of the moccasin producing a heavily puckered seam. In the Great Lakes area and to the north, a type with both vamp and toe seam was used. All forms were soft soled, with flaps covering the ankles, and in the sub-Arctic additional pieces were bound to the legs for winter protection.

Decoration of dress, ceremonial and functional objects was achieved by various media. Painting of coats from the Nascapi, Cree, Ojibwa and Métis involved intricate red and black or later multi-coloured designs, possibly symbolizing hunting tracks, caribou, canoes and toboggans drawn on with a wooden stylus. (There is also an ancient tradition of painting on rocks and cliffs in the Great Lakes and Canadian shield areas, many depicting abstract human figures, mythological spirits and monster creatures.) Porcupine and bird quills were also widely used in a number of techniques, woven, wrapped, netted or appliqué, a system of sewing quills down by folding them over and under sinew or thread stitching. Finer moosehair was commonly used by the Huron, Iroquois and Malecite, and could be stitched down or woven into a form of false embroidery. The Micmac, Huron and others used quills and moosehair on a range of bark objects made primarily for white souvenir markets, beginning as early as the 17th century. Incising, scoring and painting wood and birch bark with pictographic designs were common on containers, canoes, memory charts, grave markers, drums, vessels and boxes.

Beads from Europe largely replaced quills and hair as a decorative medium starting in the late 1600s, and by 1850 little quillwork was still being done. Most beadwork was stitched with thread on to hide or cloth in curvilinear and later floral forms to decorate articles of dress, bags, moccasins and all manner of objects, some made for the white souvenir market. The Iroquois produced masses of beadwork for sale at Niagara Falls. Other decorative media adapted from Europeans were silverwork, silk and thread embroidery on hide, and the use of ribbons of contrasting colours cut into various shapes and stitched to broadcloth. Ribbonwork had an intermittent distribution from the Atlantic to the Great Lakes. It became well developed by the Sac, Fox, Potawatomi and Winnebago, and is still popular today.

Early reports suggest that the designs used in the decoration of dress and objects had an association with the animal or spirit worlds and offered magical protection using realistic, geometrical or scroll-like designs and patterns. However, as almost nothing survives from the 16th or 17th centuries we cannot be certain of the cogent facts regarding religious symbolism, although wide use of the sun motif indicates its importance to Indian thought. The French introduced truly floral designs to the Indian 'repertoire' in about 1639 at their Indian missions in eastern Canada, and a secondary source of floral realism was probably colonial American folk art of the 18th century. Floral beadwork became very popular during the 19th century and seems to have been made by most surviving groups.

Bibliography

American Indian Art Magazine, Scottsdale, Arizona

T. J. Brasser, *'Bo'jou, Neejee!'*, National Museum of Canada

F. Denismore, *Chippewa Music*, Bureau of American Ethnology, Bulletin 45 (Washington D.C. 1910)

F. Denismore, *Chippewa Music Vol II*, Bureau of American Ethnology, Bulletin 53 (Washington D.C. 1913)

R. B. Hassrick, *The George Catlin Book of American Indians*, Promontory Press

W. R. Jacobs, *Wilderness Politics and Indian gifts: The Northern Colonial Frontier, 1748–1763*, University of Nebraska Press (Lincoln 1950)

H. McCracken, *George Catlin and the Old Frontier*, Bonanza Books

T. L. McKenney & J. Hall, *History of the Indian Tribes of North America*

McClelland & Stewart, *The Spirit Sings*, Glenbow Museum

L. H. Morgan, *League of the Iroquois*, Sage and Brother (Rochester 1851)

F. Parkman, *History of the Conspiracy of Pontiac, and the war of the North American Tribes against the English colonies after the conquest of Canada*, Little, Brown (Boston 1851)

Mah-we-do-ke-shick ('Spirit of the Skies'), a Chippewa chief, c.1860s. Note Hudson's Bay trade blanket coat, and catlinite pipe-bowl. Whitney & Zimmerman photograph.

J. R. Swanton, *The Indian Tribes of North America*, Bureau of American Ethnology, Bulletin 145 (Washington D.C. 1953)

H. H. Tanner, *Atlas of Great Lakes Indian History*, University of Oklahoma Press (Norman, Oklahoma 1987)

B. G. Trigger, *Handbook of North American Indians: Volume 15*, North-East, Smithsonian Institution, (Washington D.C. 1978)

V. Vidler, *American Indian Antiques*, A. S. Barnes & Company

P. I. Wellman, *Indian Wars and Warriors East*, Houghton Mifflin Company, Boston, The Riverside Press (Cambridge, Massachusetts 1959)

The Plates

To identify the exact source of each item reconstructed in these plates is impractical for reasons of space. All figures have been reconstructed from surviving material in museums, from contemporary paintings and drawings and from eyewitness descriptions.

A1: Virginia Algonkian man, c.1620
A Powhatan warrior, in contact (and conflict) with the Jamestown Colony. He wears a necklace of shell or bone beads.

A2: Carolina Algonkian woman, c.1580
Her buckskin skirt is the only garment worn; arms, legs, and face are painted or tattooed. The appearance of this woman, holding here a water container and ladle, is typical of those from the villages of Pomeiooc and Secotan who were in contact with the English colony at Roanoke Island in the 1580s.

A3: Niantic-Narraganset warrior, c.1670
A warrior of the 'King Philip War' period armed with a typical ball-headed club and a trade matchlock musket. Note shell necklace and wampum bead headband.

A4: Huron warrior, c.1625
Early French contacts described this wooden rod armour; note bird effigy 'gorget' ornament.

A5: Mohawk warrior, c.1640
A typical Iroquois of the 'Beaver Wars' period; these groups were usually friendly to the Dutch and English traders but hostile to the French and their Indian allies. Contemporary writings describe the striking body-painting. He holds a club with an argillite or stone head and a shaft inlaid with wampum beads.

A6: Algonkian woman, St. Lawrence Valley, c.1630
Her caribou hide tunic is decorated with porcupine quill-work. In the background are seen war posts with carved faces.

B1: Iroquois warrior, c.1759
A tattooed warrior armed with a painted trade musket; note quilled sword belt, knife sheath, moccasins, pouches and leggings.

B2: Mohawk warrior, c.1710
Note complex facial and body tattoos, ear orna-

Chippewa brave Little Shell, c.1880, probably photographed during a visit to Washington DC. Note treaty medal, and neckband of cloth probably decorated with floral beading.

ments of swan's down, and European blanket/robe and shirt. The weapon is a Hudson Valley fowling piece.

B2: Mohawk warrior, c.1764

Note feather and quillwork head ornaments, with wampum ear ornaments and 'gorget'. He carries a bow and arrows and a trade tomahawk. In the foreground, note ball-headed clubs, and red-painted scalp with decorative stretcher rim.

C1: South-eastern Ojibwa warrior, c.1800

Shirt, leggings and moccasins are of buckskin; the pouch, slung on a shoulder strap, and the knife sheath, are decorated with porcupine quill-work; the headdress is of rawhide slats wrapped round with quills and attached to a cap with various feathers. (Some feathers, such as peacock, were obtained from white traders.) He holds a wampum belt, tobacco pouch, and a warclub with an added metal trade blade.

Winnebago Indians photographed in c.1900, probably near Black River Falls, Wisconsin; photographer unknown. The men wear buckskin leggings and cloth shirts; several wear woven beaded sashes, armbands and knee-bands; second from left wears a cloth apron with abstract floral bead-work typical of the Winnebago, Potawatomi and Fox. One holds a bow and arrows, another an eagle feather fan, another a wooden warclub.

C2: Miami warrior, c.1790

He has a roach haircut, silver ear and nose ornaments (see also other figures on this plate) and silver armbands. His leggings are of buckskin, as are the pointed-flap moccasins, and the pouch with a quilled Thunderbird design.

C3: Wyandot chief, c.1780

The Wyandots were the 18th-century descendants of the 17th-century Hurons; in their new territories in the Ohio country they were allies in turn of both the French and the British. His military-style hat and coat are not cast-offs, but were produced specifically for trade. Note also native leggings, moccasins and moosehair-embroidered pouch,

45

facial paint, and German silver ornaments of impressive size.

D1: Shawnee warrior, c.1799
He wears a cloth robe and shirt, small breechcloth, buckskin leggings and moccasins, and silver ear pendants, and holds the long Woodland-style bow.

D2: Northern Ojibwa warrior, c.1780–1800
His coat of unsmoked moosehide had painted decorations; moccasins, pouch and belt are decorated with quill-work. D2a is a rear view of the same figure.

D3: Cree Women, c.1780–1800
They wear the side-seam dress known in the eastern sub-Arctic, painted with geometric and circular designs. The moccasins have large vamps but no front seams. One wears a typical cape and hood, and both have complex hair ornaments.

The Cree and Ojibwa were almost indistinguishable in many areas of the sub-Arctic.

E1: Micmac couple, c.1820
The Micmac of Nova Scotia had a long association with the French from the 16th century onwards. By the early 19th century European cloths and woollens had replaced skins for clothing, and early decorative media had been replaced by bead- and ribbon-work.

E2: Saulteaux family (north-western Ojibwa and Cree), c.1810
The canoe was indispensable for northern life, and the Ojibwa probably developed the finest examples of the craft. The man wears a cloth hood with ribbon-work decoration, the woman a 'strap-dress'. She holds her baby on a cradleboard; the cradle bag with the characteristic northern laced front is decorated with beadwork, and a quilled headbow protects the head.

E3: Details: Micmac bead-work on woman's leggings, c.1820; Micmac moccasins, c.1820; Ojibwa moccasins, c.1800.

F: Iroquois, 1800–20:
F1: Woman
She prepares corn with a pestle and mortar. Her cloth blouse and skirt are decorated with silver brooches and bead-work. Her baby hangs in a cradleboard with a cloth wrap embroidered with moosehair.

F2: Warrior, War of 1812
The buckskin coat shows European influence in its construction, and the weapon is a trade tomahawk.

F3: Dancer
He wears the 'false face', a carved mask representing a mythological being invoked to aid mankind in the elimination of disease, and holds a turtle rattle.

G1: Sac (Sauk) chief, c.1830
There was some use of the horse by Woodland tribes. Note the roach and head painting, bear claw necklace, fur cape, and extended buckskin leggings. The staff is presumably a 'coup stick'.

Back view of Lorette Huron blanket coat from the National Museum of Denmark—see Plate H3. (Drawing Richard Hook)

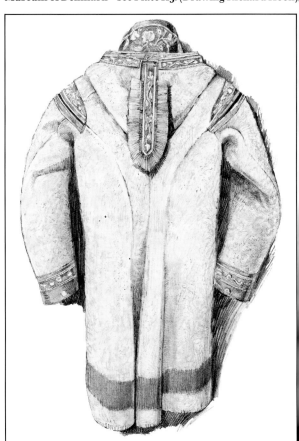

G2: Sac (Sauk) woman, c.1830
She wears a blouse decorated with silver brooches, a shawl, cloth skirt and leggings decorated with ribbon-work.

G3: Sac (Sauk) chief's son, c.1830
His buckskin shirt is similar to Plains styles; note front-seam leggings and toe-seam moccasins.

G4: Bark houses were used by the branch of the Sauk which removed to Oklahoma until *c.*1900.

G5: Ottawa chief, c.1815
He wears a blanket with appliqué decoration, trade cloth aprons, leggings, garters, and buckskin moccasins. His fur turban and cape are ornamented with stamped or cut-out silver brooches. He carries a medicine bag.

G6: Winnebago warrior, c.1820
He carries a so-called 'gunstock' warclub with a metal blade, and smoking equipment. Note peace medal; silver armbands and bracelets embellished with rattlesnake skins; and typical Winnebago moccasins with cuffs extending round the front.

H1: Menomini woman, c.1850
The satin blouse is decorated with German silver brooches, the wrap skirt and leggings with ribbon-work, and the moccasins with bead-work; note also bead necklace.

H2: Sac (Sauk) chief, c.1845
He wears a fur turban, bear claw necklace, black cloth shirt with curvilinear beaded motifs, deerskin leggings with woven bead-work, garters, moccasins, breechcloth and robe all decorated with bead- and ribbon-work. He holds a 'head-and-tail' fan, and a warclub with a metal spike.

H3: Huron-of-Lorette man, c.1845
The headdress had a cloth band with moosehair decoration and a crown of split hawk feather construction. The coat is of blanket cloth, the sash of woven wool; the cloth leggings, moccasins, pouch and mittens are largely decorated with moosehair embroidery.

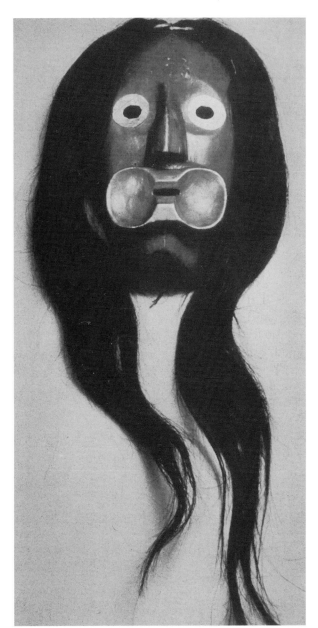

Iroquois 'False Face' mask: red and white painted wood with horsehair. This example is late 19th century, but follows a much older style. (Museum of Mankind, courtesy the Trustees of the British Museum)

H4: Southern Ojibwa (Chippewa) man, c.1865
Note feather-decorated fur turban; crossed bandolier pouches with woven bead-work, aprons and leggings of black broadcloth or velvet with floral beaded motifs. He holds a pipe with a twisted stem, and an otterskin bag. His moccasins are typical of the Southern Ojibwa, with a front seam and an instep vamp.

Notes sur les planches en couleur

A1 Un guerrier Powhatan portant un collier de coquillages ou des perles d'os. **A2** Elle porte seulement une jupe en daim et ses bras, ses jambes et son visage sont peints ou tatoués. **A3** Un guerrier de la période de la "Guerre do roi Philippe" armé d'un bâton caractéristique à bout rond et d'un mousquet à mèche qu'il a troqué. Il porte un collier de coquillages et un bandeau en perles de wampoum. **A4** Une armure à tige de bois et un ornement de gorgerin avec effigie d'oiseau. **A5** Il porte un bâton dont la tête est en argillite ou en pierre et un javelot serti en perles de wampoum. **A6** Une tunique en peau de caribou décorée avec piquants de porc-épic.

B1 Un guerrier tatoué armé d'un mousquet de troc, peint. Notez le ceinturon à piquants pour l'épée, le fourreau du couteau, les poches et les jambières. **B2** Notez les tatouages complexes sur le corps et le visage, les ornements d'oreilles en duvet de cygne et la chemise et la robe/couverture européennes. L'arme est un fusil de chasse de la vallée de l'Hudson. **B3** Parure en plumes et en piquants, ornements d'oreilles en wampoum et "gorgerin". Il porte un arc, des flèches et un tomahawk.

C1 Chemise en daim, jambières et mocassins; la bourse est portée en bandoulière sur l'épaule et le fourreau du couteau est décoré d'un ouvrage en piquants. La parure de tête est faite de lamelles de peau, de piquants et de plumes variées. Il porte une ceinture en wampoum, une blague à tabac et une massue de guerre. **C2** Coupe de cheveux en brosse, ornements d'oreilles et de nez et bandeaux sur les bras en argent, jambières en peau de daim, mocassins et sac. **C3** Le chapeau et le manteau de style militaire étaient produits spécialement pour le commerce. Jambières, mocassins et bourse de la région, peinture sur le visage et ornements allemands en argent.

D1 Robe et chemise en toile, petite bande-culotte, jambières et mocassins en daim, pendants d'oreilles en argent. Il est armé d'un long arc spécifique à la région des bois. **D2** Manteau en peau d'élan non fumée avec décorations peintes. Les mocassins, la bourse et la ceinture sont décorés de piquants. **D2a** vue arrière. **D3** Robe cousue latéralement avec dessins géométriques et circulaires, mocassins et l'un d'eux porte une cape et un capuchon caractéristiques. Tous deux ont des ornements complexes sur les cheveux.

E1 Dès le début du 19ème siècle, les étoffes et lainages européens avaient remplacé les peaux pour les vêtements et les moyens décoratifs d'autrefois étaient remplacés par les ouvrages en perles et en rubans. **E2** Cet homme porte un capuchon en toile décoré de rubans, la femme une "robe à lanières" Elle porte son enfant dans un porte-bébé. **E3** Ouvrage en perles Micmac sur les jambières de la femme, mocassins Micmac, Mocassins Ojibwa.

F1 Elle prépare du maïs avec un pilon et un mortier. La blouse et la jupe en étoffe sont décorées de broches en argent et de perles. Le bébé est suspendu dans un porte-bébé. **F2** Manteau en daim présentant une influence européenne et tomahawk de commerce. **F3** Il porte un "faux visage", un masque taillé et une crécelle en carapace de tortue.

G1 Coupe en brosse et peintures sur la tête, collier avec griffe d'ours, cape de fourrure et longues jambières en daim. Le bâton est probablement un "bâton à coup". **G2** Blouse décorée de broches en argent, un châle, une jupe en étoffe et des jambières décorées par un ouvrage de rubans. **G3** La chemise en daim est similaire aux styles des plaines; notez les jambières cousues sur le devant et les mocassins à deux coutures. **G4** Les demeures en écorce furent utilisées par la branche qui se déplaça à Oklahoma. **G5** Couverture 'avec décoration en appliqué, tabliers en toile du commerce, jambières, jarretelles et mocassins en peau de daim. Son turban et sa cape en fourrure sont décorés de broches en argent frappé ou découpé. Il porte un sac à magie, une massue de guerre dite à 'fût de fusil' avec une lame de métal, et son matériel pour fumer. Médaille de paix, bracelets et bandes d'argent sur les bras et mocassins caractéristiques des Winnebago.

H1 Blouse en satin décorée de broches en argent allemandes, jupe enroulée et jambières décorées d'un ouvrage de rubans et mocassins avec des perles; collier de perles également. **H2** Turban de fourrure, collier avec griffe d'ours, chemise en étoffe noire, jambières en peau de cerf décorées de perles, jarretelles, mocassins, bande-culotte et robe. Il tient un éventail et une massue de guerre avec une pointe de métal. **H3** Parure de tête en toile, poil d'élan et plumes de faucon. Le manteau est dans une étoffe à couverture, la ceinture de toile tissée; jambières en étoffe, mocassins, san et mitaines décorés par des broderies en poil d'élan. **H4** Turban de fourrure décoré avec une plume, sacs de bandoulière à cartouches croisée avec ouvrage en perles tissé, tabliers et jambières en toile noir large ou en velours. Pipe au tuyau tordu, et sac en peau de loutre. Mocassins caractéristiques des Ojibwa du sud.

Farbtafeln

A1 Ein Krieger von Powhatan (oder Wahunsonacock, gestorben 1618, Häuptling der Konföderation der Indianerstämme und Vater von Pocahontas) ist hier mit einer Halskette aus Muscheln oder Knochen abgebildet. **A2** Sie trägt nur einen Wildlederrock und ihre Arme, Beine und ihr Gesicht sind bemalt oder tätowiert. **A3** Krieger aus der "King Philip"-Kriegszeit (ca.1670), bewaffnet mit Kugelkopfkeule und handelsüblicher Luntenschloßmuskete. Er hat eine Muschelhalskette und ein Muschelperlen-Kopfband. **A4** Holzstabbewaffnung und eine Vogelplastik-'Gorget'-Verzierung. **A5** Er hält in der Hand eine Keule mit Ton- oder Steinspitze, deren Griff mit Muschelperlen eingelegt ist. **A6** Eine Karibuledertunika verziert mit den Stacheln des Stachelschweins.

B1 Ein Krieger mit tätowierten Armen und einer bemalten handelsüblichen Muskete. Auffallend sind der mit Stacheln besetzte Schwertgürtel, die Messerhülle, Mokassins, Taschen und Leggins. **B2** Zu beachten sind die ausführlichen Gesichts- und Körpertätowierungen, Der Ohrschmuck aus Schwanenfedern, sowie die europäische Decke/Umhang und das Hemd. Die Waffe ist eine 'Hudson-Valley'-Vogelflinte. **B3** Kopfschmuck aus Federn und Stacheln, Ohrschmuck aus Muschelperlen und 'Gorget'. Er Besitzt Pfeil, Bogen und Tomahawk.

C1 Wildlederrock, Leggins und Mokassins. Das Schulterband der Umhängetasche sowie die Messerhülle sind mit Stacheln verziert. Die Kopfbedeckung wurde aus Rohleder, Stacheln und verschiedenen Federn hergestellt. Er Hält einen Muschelperlengürtel, Tabaktasche und ein Kriegsbeil. **C2** Bogenförmiger Haarschnitt, silberner Ohr- und Nasenschmuck, sowie Armbänder, Leggins, Mokassins und Tasche. **C3** Hut und Mantel im Militärstil wurden besonders für den Handel angefertigt. Ursprüngliche Leggins, Mokassins und Tasche, Gesichtsbemalung und Neusilberschmuck.

D1 Stoffgewand un -hemd, kleiner Lendenschurz, Leggins und Mokassins, silberner Ohranhänger. Er ist mit einem langen, in den Wäldern üblichen Bogen bewaffnet. **D2** Der Mantel ist aus ungeräuchertem Elchleder und bemalt. Mokassins, Tasche und Gürtel sind mit Stacheln verziert. **D2a** Rückansicht. **D3** Bekleidung mit Seitennaht, geometrischen und runden Entwürfen, Mokassins und der typische Umhang mit Kapuze. Beide tragen umfrangreichen Haarschmuck.

E1 Zu Beginn des 19. Jahrhunderts ersetze europäische Bekleidung aus Stoff und Wolle das übliche Leder. Andere Verzierungsmaterialien wurden durch Ketten- und Schnürarbeiten ersetzt. **E2** Der Mann trägt einen, mit Schnüren verzierten Hut, die Frau trägt ein Riemenkleid. Ihr Baby liegt in einer Art Wiege. **E3** 'Micmac'-Perlenarbeit auf den Frauenleggins, 'Micmac'-Mokassins, 'Ojibwa'-Mokassins.

F1 Sie bereitet Mais mit Mörset und Stößel zu. Stoffbluse und -hemd sind mit Silberspangen und Perlenarbeit verziert. Das Baby liegt in einer hängenden Wiege. **F2** Der Wildledermantel zeigt europäischen Einfluß; sowie das handelsübliche Tomahawk. **F3** Er trägt ein "falsches Gesicht", eine geschnizte Maske un hält eine Schildpattrassel in der Hand.

G1 Bogenförmiger Haarschnitt mit Kopfbemalung, Bärenkrallen-Halskette, Pelzumhang und verlängerte Leggins. Der Stab ist wohl ein 'Coup Stick'. **G2** Eine, mit Silberspangen Verzierte Bluse, ein Schal, ein Stoffrock und Leggins verziert mit Schnürarbeit. **G3** Das Wildlederhemd ist dem einfacheren Stil ähnlich; auffallend ist die Vordernaht der Leggins und die Werggarnnaht der Mokassins. **G4** Häuser aus Baumrinde wurden von einem Zweig der Sauk Verwendet, die nach Oklahoma zogen. **G5** Decke mit Applikationsstickerei, handelsübliche Stoffschürzen, Leggins, Gamaschen und Wildledermokassins. Sein Pelzturban und Umhang wurde bedruckt mit mit ausgeschnittenen Silberspangen verziert. Er besitzt eine Medizintasche. **G6** Er besitzt ein 'Gunstock'-Kriegsbeil mit Metallklinge, sowie Rauchausrüstung. Friedensmedaille, Silberarmbänder und Ketten sowie die typischen Winnebago Mokassins.

H1 Satinbluse mit Neusilberspangen verziert; Wickelrock und Leggins haben Schnürarbeit und die Mokassins sind mit Perlen versehen; außerdem eine Perlen-Halskette. **H2** Pelzturban, Bärenkrallen-Halskette, schwarzes Stoffhemd, Hirschleder-Leggins mit Perlenarbeit, Gamaschen, Mokassins, Lendenschurz und Umhang. Er hält einen 'Kopf-und-Schwanz' Fecher sowie ein Kriegsbeil mit metallspitze. **H3** Kopfbedeckung aus Stoff, Elchshaaren und Adlerfedern. Der Mantel ist aus Deckenstoff, die Kordel aus gewebtem Stoff; Stoff-Leggins, Mokassins, Tasche und Handschuhe sind mit Elchshaarstickerei versehen. **H4** Pelzturban mit Federn Verziert, Bandoliertasche mit gewebter Kettenarbeit, Schürzen und Leggins aus schwarzem, feinem Wollstoff oder Samt. Pfeife mit geschwungenem Stil und einer Otterfelltasche. Typische südliche Ojibwa Mokassins.